William M. Clarke

How the City of London Works

An Introduction to its Financial Markets

3rd Edition

WATERLOW PUBLISHERS

First Edition 1986
2nd Edition 1988
3rd Edition 1991
Reprinted 1993
Reprinted 1994
© W. M. Clarke 1986, 1988, 1991

Published by
Sweet and Maxwell Limited of
South Quay Plaza, 183 Marsh Wall, London E14 9FT;
Formerly published by
Waterlow Publishers

ISBN 0 08 040867 2

British Library Cataloguing in Publication Data

Clarke, William M. (*William Malpas, 1922–*)
How the City of London works: an
introduction to its financial markets.
3rd ed.
1. Financial institutions
——London (City)
I. Title
332.1'09421'2

—

Designed by the Graphic Partnership
Printed in Great Britain by
BPC Wheatons Ltd, Exeter

By the Same Author

Planning for Europe: 1992
The Secret Life of Wilkie Collins
Inside the City
The World's Money
Britain's Invisible Earnings
Private Enterprise in Developing Countries
The City in the World Economy
The City's Invisible Earnings

Preface

The aim of this small guide is to explain quite simply what goes on in the financial markets of the City of London and how each of them works. It is intended, therefore, as a helpful companion to the stream of other books on the City's activities.

It is not concerned with the arguments about the City: whether it does harm to the economy or whether it is the saviour of Britain's balance of payments. It is in essence a 'child's guide' (in words, diagrams and pictures) to the score of markets and specialisations that make up London's financial centre.

This completely revised edition covers various major changes arising not only from 'Big Bang' in October 1986 and from the stock market 'crash'of October 1987, but from more recent developments well into 1991.

I am indebted to all the leading City institutions and associations for the helpful provision of both material and time in the preparation of this small book. Some individuals have helped more than most. Among them are Christopher Biggs of the City Communications Centre, who was a continuous support in the early stages; Jasmine Boxall and Sheila Tunnacliffe who became deeply immersed in the proofs; and James Lamb whose enthusiasm for the whole project never flagged. To Savills go my special thanks for providing the information for the City of London distribution maps.

W.M.C.
May 1991

Contents

To Deborah, Pamela, Evan and Noel

1. What the City Does

Where it is

Before trying to describe how the City works, let's first establish where it is. As its nickname suggests, it covers no more than a square mile (actually 274 hectares) and is roughly synonymous with the local authority area of the Corporation of London.

It is hardly a square, more an odd-shaped rectangle, stretching from the Law Courts at one end to the Tower of London at the other, and from the north bank of the Thames in the south to the outskirts of the Barbican and Liverpool Street Station, in the north.

Within its narrow area, the various markets and specialisations cluster in quite separate spots, banking here, insurance there, commodities here, shipping over there. Yet none is far from the others. It is possible to walk from one end of the City to the other in under twenty minutes and most of the main sections are within five minutes' walk of each other.

Where then to start? The obvious spot is Bank tube station. As one emerges from the exit in front of the Royal Exchange steps one is at the heart of the financial district. The Royal Exchange, home in the course of its four hundred year history of Lloyd's, the foreign exchange market and several commodity markets, now houses Guardian Royal Exchange, one of the oldest of the insurance companies.

Over on the left is the entrance to the Bank of England. A little beyond in the same direction rises the Stock Exchange tower. Immediately behind one is the Mansion House, home (literally) of the Lord Mayor. And, within two hundred yards in different directions, stand the headquarters of the big clearing banks: Lloyds (on the right, just across Cornhill), Barclays, Midland, National Westminster and the London office of the Royal Bank of Scotland.

This, therefore, is the hub of the financial district, with various spokes of the wheel leading off to the commodity markets, between

Fenchurch Street and Eastcheap, the insurance broking world, extending from Leadenhall Street and Lime Street towards Aldgate, the shipping community around Leadenhall Street and St. Mary Axe, and the discount houses close to Lombard Street, with foreign banks clustered down Gresham Street, Moorgate and now Eastcheap.

What it does

The phrase 'the City of London' is employed as useful shorthand to describe the financial (and commercial) institutions in the Square Mile; and, like all shorthand phrases, it leaves out a great deal. It should not imply that other cities in the United Kingdom do not have similar institutions. Nor should it leave the impression that most people employed in finance actually work in London (in fact, only about a fifth do so).

Bank branches operate in most high streets. So do thousands of insurance company branches, insurance brokers and unit trust offices. Edinburgh rivals London as the hub of the investment trust world and Birmingham, Manchester, Liverpool, Leeds, Newcastle and Bristol are commercial centres in their own right.

What then distinguishes London from the rest? Fundamentally it is that the main financial markets operate in the Square Mile and that the head offices of most financial institutions are still located there. It is also the home of the Government's main monetary arm, the Bank of England, and the place where foreign financial institutions choose to place their representatives.

For all these reasons, London's markets and institutions attract the bulk of the country's savings, investments and money decisions in general. Thus the City is like some huge magnet, pulling the results of activities in Manchester, Birmingham or even Hong Kong or Rio to a narrow spot in London, whether they relate to foreign exchange, rubber, shipping freights, satellite risks, Government securities, or just the payment of a bill by cheque. In one way or another, the City's mechanism comes into play.

London's Markets

Let us be more precise. A good many people, in the course of their working life, make contributions to their future pensions on a regular basis. Their employer, who will also be making a contribution, will have a pension fund to receive such contributions and to invest the money as it accumulates. How is this done? The fund will have an investment manager who in turn will use a stockbroker or merchant banker to help him choose and purchase industrial shares, gilt-edged stock or even foreign securities. Such transactions will ultimately lead to the purchase of existing, or sometimes newly issued, stock in the stock market. So at the end of the chain, a transaction takes place in the market place in the City of London.

Also consider the sale of British machinery in Lancashire to a foreign importer in Mexico. The transaction will need to be financed, insured and shipped. A local bank in Manchester will arrange export finance through its foreign branch in London; insurance may be arranged through a London-based company; and the shipping arrangements may eventually be secured on the Baltic Exchange in St. Mary Axe. City institutions, not a stone's throw from each other, enable the transaction to be completed.

Finally take an endowment policy taken out with a life insurance office in Norwich, Salisbury or Gloucester. The premiums will be paid annually. The life office needs to invest the money until either a death claim is made or the policy matures; and it will consider a number of options: buying industrial equities or Government securities; purchasing farmland or property; investing abroad in existing shares or in a wide range of venture enterprises. The decisions to do one or the other will inevitably take place in the life company's London office and that office, in turn, will use the appropriate City market for its purposes: the stock market to buy securities; the foreign exchange market to transfer funds abroad for foreign investment or to cover some of its risks; even the new financial futures market to cover some of its other risks.

To sum Up

Once again a small transaction in the provinces has led to the use of markets or specialisations in the City. We shall discover more examples as we go along. But, at this early stage, let us try to sum up what the City, in its broadest sense, seems to do:

(i) It enables monetary payments to be made from one person (or company) to another.

(ii) It enables payments to be made across frontiers to and from any country in the world.

(iii) It attracts investment funds from all parts of the United Kingdom and overseas and, through its markets and contacts, provides a means of investing them in securities, industrial plant, property, farmland, commodities or gold.

(iv) It provides the means of financing trade, industry and government projects on a national or world-wide basis.

3

(v) It offers a variety of financial and commercial services on an international scale, from insurance to shipping freights and from investment advice to legal advice.

In short, it will save, invest, finance, insure, ship, trade, buy, sell or hedge for you, me, or anyone else, on a world-wide basis. How it does so, we must begin to explore in the next chapter.

The City's 'Canary Wharf' Extension

The fiscal attractions offered by the Docklands Development Corporation and the possible shortage of large office spaces in the City itself have combined to produce a potential extension of the City at Canary Wharf, two miles east of the City. The £4 billion development, seen through to fruition by Olympia & York, is filling up with British and, mainly, American financial institutions. The 800-foot, 50-storey tower, Britain's tallest, has already become a feature of the City's eastern skyline, and is capable of housing 11,500 office workers. Present expansion plans, if they come to fruition by the mid-1990s, will be able to supply up to 10 million square feet of office space, equivalent to a fifth of the space in the City of London.

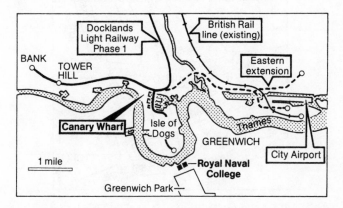

Some people believe it will shift the City's centre of gravity eastwards and create similar transport problems in London to those faced by visiting bankers in New York, in coping with offices in both Lower Manhattan and Park Avenue. More likely, the City's 'decision-making' fulcrum will remain around the Bank of England and Canary Wharf will become an exciting, integrated extension of the City's new market-dealing floor technology.

Where To See The City At Work

The following walk through the City, calling at the main markets, is designed to provide a visual impression of what the City really stands for: active markets in money, goods and services. They provide the same colour, bustle and noise of markets anywhere, with one major difference: the prices are rather higher.

Several parts of the City and its markets can still be visited. But it is no longer the easy arrangement it used to be. Some City markets, such as the new Lloyd's building, can and will cope with large numbers of visitors. Others, such as the Bank of England Museum, the London Metal Exchange, the Baltic Exchange, cannot. The London Stock Exchange is at present closed to visitors. So appointments and forward planning are essential.

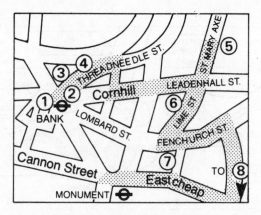

WE START AT BANK UNDERGROUND STATION.

⬇

(1) Mansion House

The Mansion House is the official residence of the Lord Mayor of London. It is also the venue for much of the City's hospitality where guests such as the Prime Minister, Chancellor of the Exchequer, foreign Heads of State, etc. are invited to official banquets. The building was started in 1738 and completed in 1752. The Lord Mayor is titular head of the Corporation of London, the City's governing body, which is responsible through its elected members for the administration of the City, providing, in essence, the infrastructure for the financial sector.

⬇

(2) Royal Exchange

In the past, the Royal Exchange has housed the City's foreign exchange market and Lloyd's. At present it is the home of the Guardian Royal Exchange and also the London International Financial Futures Exchange. The present building was opened by Queen Victoria on 28th October 1844. Royal Exchange Assurance, now merged in Guardian Royal Exchange, have occupied the building (and its two predecessors) since 1720. The London International Financial Futures Exchange, which has occupied the area of the courtyard and ambulatory since September 1982, will be moving to the River Building at the new Cannon Bridge Development.

⬇

(3) Bank of England

Founded in 1694, the Bank of England did not move into Threadneedle Street until 1734. The nickname 'The Old Lady of Threadneedle Street' was first used in James Gillroy's cartoon of 1797. The Bank expanded to cover the present site between 1765 and 1833, and was finally rebuilt by Sir Herbert Baker between 1925 and 1939. In the vaults are the nation's gold reserves.

⬇

(4) London Stock Exchange

The Stock Exchange has its origins in the sixteenth century and as the scale of commercial activity has increased, especially in the last 150 years, the Exchange has expanded to handle the increased demand for capital. Today over 7,000 securities are listed on The London Stock Exchange with a turnover of £1,666,600 million in 1990. The present building was opened by the Queen in November 1972.

⬇

(5) Baltic Exchange

The Baltic Exchange is a unique international shipping exchange. Its members comprise merchants, shipowners, shipbrokers and some other

companies associated with shipping. About 2,000 persons have a right
of entry to the 'Floor' of the Exchange, where a freight market is held
daily and cargo ships are chartered by brokers acting for merchants
from all over the world. Vessels are bought and sold on behalf of
clients, while other members trade in grains, edible oils and oilseeds.
The present building was completed in 1903.

(6) Lloyd's

Lloyd's of London is an international insurance market. Insurance
risks are placed with individual underwriting members who have
personal and unlimited liability. Currently, there are over 26,500
members divided into some 345 syndicates. Business from all parts of
the world is placed at Lloyd's through the 260 authorised firms of
Lloyd's brokers. Its new building was officially opened in November
1986.

(7) London Metal Exchange

The London Metal Exchange is an international terminal market
where copper, lead, zinc, tin, aluminium and nickel are traded in
standard units of guaranteed quality. Trade is conducted inter-office
and by open outcry, the latter involving the 7 Ring firms whose
representatives call out their offers for sale and bids to buy in four
sessions each day. The market is at present in the Plantation House
complex.

(8) London Futures and Options Exchange (London FOX)

The London Futures and Options Exchange is a major international
centre for the trading of soft commodities. These include cocoa,
robusta coffee, raw and white sugar, potatoes, grain, soya bean meal,
arabica coffee, rice, meat and the MGMI. The Exchange is located in
St. Katherine's Dock. In January 1991 London FOX took over the
administration of the Baltic Futures Markets following a merger of the
two exchanges.

RETURN TO MONUMENT UNDERGROUND STATION.

List of Addresses and Contact Points

(1) Mansion House and Guildhall

Specialist groups may be shown round Mansion House, Guildhall, and Barbican Estate. Visits to certain livery companies may also be arranged. Applications stating individual requirements, should be made direct to the City Guide at Guildhall.
The Mansion House will close from 1991 to 1993 for rebuilding.

Where to Write:
City Guide
Public Relations Department
Guildhall
London EC2P 2EJ
Tel: 071-606 3030

(2) LIFFE

Members of the public may, by application, view the London International Financial Futures Exchange from the Visitors' Gallery, entrance nearest to Bank Underground station. They will receive a short talk on the functions and operations of LIFFE. Applications should be made to the Visitors' Gallery Co-ordinator at LIFFE.

Note: LIFFE has announced its intention to merge its operations with the London Traded Options Market by the end of 1991. The combined new exchange is then expected to move to the River Building at the new Cannon Bridge development.

Where to Write:
The Visitors' Gallery
Co-ordinator
LIFFE Ltd
Royal Exchange
London EC3V 3PJ
Tel: 071-623 0444

(3) Bank of England Museum

Educational presentations take place in the Bank of England's Museum cinema (entrance in Bartholomew Lane), and are for groups of between 12 and 30 people, although smaller groups may be accepted in exceptional circumstances. The groups catered for are:

(1) *5–10-year-olds*. A 45–60 minute presentation is given, taking the audience on a trip through time, stopping to look at different systems of exchange and money. There will be some audience participation and a 15-minute cartoon film, *The Curious History of Money*. Allow 2 hours for visit.

(2) *11–14-year-olds*. A 45–60 minute presentation is given, looking in very simple terms at the qualities of money, including colour slides and a cartoon film. Allow $1\frac{1}{2}$ hours for visit.

(3) *15–18-year-olds*. A half-hour presentation is given, consisting of video modules interspersed with speaker/slide sections, followed by a question and answer session. Alternatively, a 30-minute film can be seen.

(4) *General interest*. A 40-minute slide show can be seen, covering the history of the Bank of England. There is also a 40-minute film and slide presentation covering a brief history of English banknotes and their complete production process.

Where to Write:
Public Liaison Group
Information Division
Bank of England
Threadneedle Street
London EC2R 8AH
Tel: 071-601 4878

(4) London Stock Exchange

The Stock Exchange closed for public viewing in 1990.

Where to Write:
Investor Research and
Education
The London
Stock Exchange
London EC2N 1HP
Tel: 071-588 2355

(5) Baltic Exchange

Educational visits to the Exchange, by appointment only,
Monday to Friday at 11.30 a.m. and 12.30 p.m.
Maximum number in a party is 20; minimum age 17.

Where to Write:

The Secretary
The Baltic Exchange
19/21 Bury St
London EC3A 5AU
Tel: 071-623 5501

(6) Lloyd's

Visitors may trace the history of Lloyd's with the help of
models and videos before viewing the Underwriting Room
from one of the galleries surrounding the central atrium.
Assistants are available to talk to groups about the workings
of the Room and answer questions. Admission is between
9.30 a.m. and 12.30 p.m. and 2.00 p.m. to 4.00 p.m. for
pre-booked groups of four or more people only, Monday to
Friday. There is no admission charge.

Where to Write:

Visits Section
Public Affairs Department
Lloyd's of London
1 Lime Street
London EC3M 7HA
Tel: 071-327 6210/5286

(7) London Metal Exchange

The public may arrange to watch the 'Ring' by appointment.
Most visits are from 12 noon to 1.00 p.m. and video
presentations are available. Parties should number no more
than 15. Only one educational visit per week can be
accommodated and those taking part must be of at least 'A' level
standard.

Where to Write:

Brian Reidy & Associates
Suite 144, 7th floor
Plantation House
Fenchurch Street
London EC3M 3AP
Tel: 071-283 3617
        071-626 1828

(8) London Futures and Options Exchange (London FOX)

Visits can be arranged once a month by appointment for business
or educational groups to view the markets while trading is in
progress.

Where to Write:

Marketing Manager
London Futures and Options
Exchange
1 Commodity Quay
St. Katherine's Dock
London E1 9AX
Tel: 071-481 2080

2. Banking

What is Money?

Money is at the heart of the City, and so are the banks which deal in money and, to some extent, even create it.

In order to know what a bank is and does, therefore, we need to know a little about the developments in the use of money: how in brief we managed to move from barter to the creation of credit. This was, of course, achieved in two basic stages. First came the transition from barter to the use of shells, beads and gold as a means of exchange: that is, the creation of acceptable, though often primitive, money. This in turn led to the establishment of coins and, much later, paper notes by governments and, more recently, to the use of telephonic and electronic transfers of money. The second stage, which overlapped the first, was the jump from an acceptable means of exchange to the creation of credit; and then, in progression, to the use of cheques, credit cards and home banking by television.

Let us begin with money itself. As the textbooks always tell us, money is simply an *acceptable* means of exchange that can be measured in small units, and used as a stable store of value. The key word is acceptable. People must be willing to accept the means of exchange, whether beads, shells or paper notes, knowing that when the time comes to exchange them, in their turn, for something else, their value will be universally recognised.

A bank is not necessary for this basic mechanism of exchange. What a bank is useful for (though not entirely necessary for, as we shall see in a moment) is the next step in development: the creation of credit. Historically, credit creation can be pushed back as far as the Florentines in the 15th century. But it was being undertaken on a regular basis by the goldsmiths by the end of the seventeenth century; they were well-established as safe havens not only for bullion, but jewellery and cash. They had also begun to do something else, which was to have a much wider significance: they started to issue receipts for such deposits and to lend some of the wealth left with them to others.

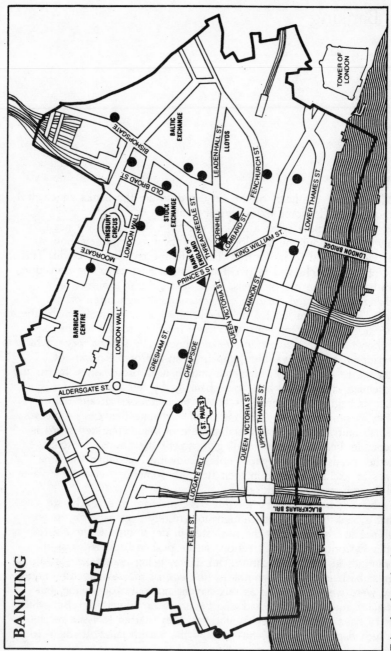

BANKING

TOWER OF LONDON

BISHOPSGATE
BALTIC EXCHANGE
OLD BROAD ST
LEADENHALL ST
LLOYDS
FENCHURCH ST
FINSBURY CIRCUS
STOCK EXCHANGE
LONDON WALL
MOORGATE
THREADNEEDLE ST
BANK OF ENGLAND
CORNHILL
LOMBARD ST
KING WILLIAM ST
LONDON BRIDGE
LOWER THAMES ST
PRINCE'S ST
QUEEN VICTORIA ST
CANNON ST
BARBICAN CENTRE
LONDON WALL
GRESHAM ST
CHEAPSIDE
ALDERSGATE ST.
ST. PAUL'S
QUEEN VICTORIA ST
UPPER THAMES ST
LUDGATE HILL
FLEET ST
BLACKFRIARS BRI.

Triangles show the clearing banks' head offices and circles merchant banks (source: Savills City Office Research Department)

The receipts rapidly developed into bank notes and the lending of the deposited money (at least up to certain proportions which they learned to be safe) took them into banking as we now know it. They were, in essence, judging how much of their basic deposits would be needed soon, and lending the rest to people whom they felt were credit-worthy.

But one need not seek such credit-creating examples in history. Just consider what happened in Ireland's pubs when the banks closed during a prolonged strike in the 1960's. Here is a contemporary description by Lord Kilbracken of one Irish village, Killeshandra:

'The first thing that happened was that most grocers and almost all pubs became bankers overnight. They were taking lots of money which they didn't like keeping in cash.

'So they were happy to change cheques much more readily than usual. They also made many arrangements with local factories and offices which took no cash but required it for wages.

'The money taken across the counter at Looney's Bar was sent down the road to pay the wages at O'Rourke's factory.

'Then things went a stage further. Looney would receive in return O'Rourke's unencashable cheque. But the credit standing of Seamus O'Rourke is good, and it would be accepted by the wholesaler in payment of Looney's account.

'The wholesaler, in return, would pass it on, till eventually it might find its way back to Seamus, who could happily tear it up.'

So a nation managed to live on existing credit (cheques circulated through pubs, grocers etc.) for several months without a bank being open. Whether it could have continued to do so much longer, without a major disaster, is open to doubt. The example simply serves to show that, even without a bank, credit is based on acceptability, trust and the judgement of credit-worthiness.

What is a Bank?

We can now return to the real banking world, and reconsider what a bank is and does. Amazingly, despite London being regarded as a major banking centre, no definition existed of a bank prior to 1979. At that time a Banking Act was passed resulting from the secondary banking collapse of the 1970s. The Act defined a bank and established a two-tier status. The largest banks, providing a comprehensive range of services, were known as recognised banks, whilst smaller and more specialised institutions were known as licensed deposit takers. The 1979 Banking Act made it illegal for anybody not authorised to accept deposits from the general public. The two-tier system was abolished by the Banking Act 1987 and now there is a single category of 'authorised institutions' which can vary from Barclays Bank to the financial subsidiary of Marks and Spencer.

How then does a bank move from that first step of the acceptance of a monetary deposit from the public to the creation of credit? If it wishes to survive it will wish to invest its first deposits in ways that secure a steady income and still enable it to pay back its depositors on demand, or when agreed. This will persuade it to lend some of it on a day-to-day basis in the money market and to acquire short-term Government bonds. It will also, particularly if it is a High Street bank, leave some on deposit at the Bank of England—the equivalent of cash. All this ensures that its essential 'liquidity' (that is, its ability to turn the investments into cash quickly) remains high.

Over time the banks will have learnt that some depositors are longer-term than others and, like the goldsmiths, they will consider on-lending some of these deposits to commercial borrowers. Thus begins the pyramid of credit creation we are all familiar with.

In fact, when a bank agrees to make a loan it does not usually dole out the whole amount in cash. The borrower is able to overdraw his normal account (made up of the money he has deposited with the bank) by the use of a cheque book. These cheques will, in their turn, be deposited in a bank. As a result, unless an overdraft is being repaid, total deposits are increased as a result of the new loan. Loans are created in more direct ways too.

Similarly if a bank buys securities it will provide a cheque in exchange and this too will eventually be deposited in a bank. Here again total deposits will have been increased. Thus both new loans and the purchase of new securities often lead to the creation of deposits. These are just examples of the way in which deposits can be created by individual banks. The process also embraces the banking system as a whole.

The only brake on this magical process, apart from the Bank of England's constant supervision, is of course, the banks' fear that its original depositors (as well as the new ones) will want their money back in the form of cash. If they did, there would be what is known as a 'run on the bank', customers rushing to get their money back at the same time. To avoid this banks have learned to maintain a certain level of cash (in notes and coins or with the Bank of England) or other liquid assets which can be turned into cash quickly.

We can now see how and why a bank uses its resources in a variety of ways, keeping some in cash or 'near-cash' (i.e. a deposit at the Bank of England), investing some short-term in bills or loans to the money market, investing some in Government securities of varying lengths, and lending some to personal and corporate borrowers.

14

What banks offer

So far we have explained that banks receive deposits and invest and lend the proceeds. These different processes now need to be explained in a little more detail.

The reasons why banks receive deposits are not far to seek. A current account, on which until recently the customer never received any interest, provides him with the means of making payments swiftly and efficiently, by the use of cheques, standing orders or credit transfers. A deposit account is a way of keeping money safe, and, at the same time, earning interest. Banks now offer a variety of options to depositors, varying from bank to bank, and ranging from small savings and budget accounts to so-called deposit accounts for especially large sums. They also entice customers with a variety of services, from the safeguarding of valuables (shades of the goldsmiths) to executor and trustee services.

There is one further source of deposits which needs to be sketched in before we turn to the uses banks make of them. Until about fifteen years ago, the main High Street banks relied almost entirely on normal short-term deposits for their various lending activities. But with the abolition of their agreed rates of interest (at which each bank received deposits) they were able to compete individually for large sums of money from other financial institutions and elsewhere. From that moment onwards each bank offered to pay its own agreed rates of interest over agreed periods. On this basis a new highly competitive inter-bank money market was established. It was, in effect, a large wholesale money market and enabled the banks to offer medium-term loans. With some money lent to them for longer periods, the banks were able to offer loans for longer periods too.

Let us now turn to the use made of all these deposits. We have already touched on the various ways in which the banks invest their money in the money market, the gilt-edged market and the Bank of England. We shall be explaining exactly how they do this and what effect it has on official monetary policy when we look at the operations of the money market in chapter 7.

This brings us to their lending policies and the different methods they use to provide loans to customers. This can best be tackled by brief descriptions of what they offer.

Overdrafts The overdraft is the traditional method of obtaining short-term funds for personal convenience or, in business, often to finance stocks or work in progress. The customer agrees a maximum limit with his bank and can then draw on his own account up to this amount, being charged only on what he uses at the current rate of interest. The overdraft has flexibility, for the bank and customer, but it

15

is also repayable on demand. Although banks normally agree to 'roll over' overdrafts (i.e. to lengthen the term of the loan, after appropriate reviews, by extensions), it is not a satisfactory way of providing industry with longer-term certainty.

Term Loans These are basically for a fixed amount, for a fixed period (say seven to ten years though sometimes up to 25 or 30 years) and at a fixed or variable rate of interest for the purchase of fixed assets such as premises or machinery. The borrower can receive the whole amount at once or draw it down gradually and naturally pays for it from the first day. The borrower does not have the full flexibility provided by an overdraft, though he can still choose when he needs the money. He has the advantage of knowing it is his for the agreed period and he can plan accordingly. It is worth noting that a contractual loan of this kind can also be for a short period.

Consumer Finance Whilst overdrafts have been the traditional method of obtaining finance from a bank, tremendous growth has been seen in the provision to private customers of packaged lending. This consists of personal loans, revolving credit accounts and budget accounts and in addition many banks are moving towards formal overdraft arrangements linked to income levels and renewable on an annual basis.

All the banks provide credit card facilities to customers and non-customers alike. The major networks of Access and Visa currently boast over 28m. cards issued and as at the end of 1989 an outstanding balance of over £7bn. Banks have also encroached on the traditional business of building societies, house mortgage lending. They now have some 29% of the total mortgage market and this percentage is increasing steadily.

Financial Services As the financial markets have been deregulated, the banks have diversified into the provision of a vast range of financial services. Banks today represent a substantial proportion of new insurance policies and unit trusts sold. This has accorded with the development of their merchant banking and investment banking subsidiaries following the deregulation of the Stock Exchange in 1986.

Export Credits Financing international trade, through the use of the traditional overdraft (see p. 15) or the acceptance credit (see p. 18), has been the accepted role of the banks for well over a century. The clearing banks, however, moved into the financing of

The Banking Habit in Britain

More and more people have opened bank accounts and adopted the banking habit. The proportion of the working population with a current account has risen from just over 50 per cent in 1976 to 95 per cent. More people are being paid their wages and salaries through their bank accounts:

	1976	1983	1989
Proportion of working population with a current account	51%	75%	95%
Proportion of employees paid through banks	39%	56%	77%

Britain's High Street banks now:

● serve some 58 million bank accounts.

● have deposits worth £100 billion.

● handle over 5 billion payments a year.

● employ over 400,000 people.

The services the public have been receiving from the banks have been changing even more rapidly than the growth of customers. They have been spurred on by the use and versatility of new technology. Computerisation is reducing paperwork. The use of cheques is now in decline (a drop of 40 per cent is expected over the next decade) as plastic cards take on more of the burden. After credit cards have come debit cards, designed to automate retail shopping through EFTPOS (electronic funds transfer at point of sale).

These developments have enabled the banks to emphasise, and cater for, different customer needs, extending from retail financial services, including counselling advice, to business development needs.

overseas trade only this century. The variations are now both sophisticated and almost bewildering. In some areas of the world the basic re-assurance needed by banks providing such credits is invariably a Government guarantee covering the political (and allied credit) risk. If the exporter has taken out an insurance policy with the Export Credits Guarantee Department (ECGD), and assigned it to the bank concerned, it provides collateral for the essential credit.

Bills of Exchange   These have been the traditional instrument used in international trade for centuries. A bill is in effect a promise to pay a given sum on a given date and will often be provided by an importer, while he awaits delivery of the goods. The exporter who receives such a bill can negotiate an overdraft or credit facility with a bank or can discount it, that is sell it to the bank at a discount: another alternative is for the importer to ask his local bank to open what is called a documentary acceptance credit in favour of the exporters; the bank thus promises to accept a bill of exchange accompanied by shipping documents. Acceptance credits have traditionally been offered as a form of short-term credit by London's accepting houses (another word for the merchant banks), when they 'accept' bills of exchange. This means that they guarantee payment of the bill on the due date, in return for a commission. Such bank bills (i.e. with the name of a bank on them) can be discounted in the money market, that is sold at a discount to the discount houses or 'bill brokers'.

Factoring   Exporters or other traders with trade debts of varying kinds can offer them to a bank providing factoring services and receive various services. The bank (or factoring subsidiary) will relieve the exporter of the debt anxieties, provide a sales ledger accounting service and act as debt-collector. The exporter will often be provided with cash for his day-to-day needs.

Leasing   Banks, or their leasing subsidiaries, finance the acquisition of equipment, machinery, vehicles etc, through leasing. This means that the assets concerned are hired out, at agreed rates, to the borrowing company but remain in the ownership of the bank or leasing company and revert to them at the end of the agreed period of the lease. Leasing companies (or the banks involved) sometimes provide servicing and maintenance.

Forfaiting   This is a form of supplier's credit ranging from six months to five years and above. The mechanism used is the purchase of bills of exchange or promissory notes (rather like IOU's) by the bank in cases where the piece of paper is evidence of deferred trade debt. The bills or notes are usually arranged to mature at six monthly intervals. The bill (or IOU) is regarded as a firm obligation on the part of the importer to pay.

Venture capital   The financing of small or new growth enterprises has now expanded into an activity with its own association (the British Venture Capital Association). It is in essence risk capital coupled with expertise. Venture capital can be a combination of equity and fixed interest loans, but the expertise now provided encompasses also acquisitions and management buy-outs (MBOs). The aim behind such financial support for the bank or institution concerned is to enable a small or new company to grow rapidly enough to be sold or floated on an appropriate securities market.

What Merchant Banks Do

London's merchant banks have proved to be some of the more flexible of the City's institutions. Their clients remain world wide. But the services they offer have continued to reflect current conditions. They no longer have the financial muscle of the nineteenth century. The deposit-raising abilities of the clearing banks have dwarfed the amounts the merchant banks can raise from their own resources. But their contacts, expertise and flexibility have assured their survival and prosperity. The main merchant banks retain the names of their founders (e.g. Kleinwort Benson, Morgan Grenfell, Hambro, Rothschild, Warburg, Schroder, Lazard, Baring etc.), some from the eighteenth century, some the nineteenth and some from the post-war period. The clearing banks have either acquired old established merchant banks or created their own. So have the leading foreign and overseas banks. Mergers with security houses have enlarged their activities since 'Big Bang'. The merchant banks (or investment banks as they are known in other centres) basically undertake wholesale banking business for large industrial and private clients and for Governments and their agencies. Their main areas of activity remain as follows:

- *Banking services*: ranging from the traditional acceptance credit (including a variety of credits for export business and large international projects) to foreign exchange business.

- *Corporate finance*: offering advice to large corporations on acquisitions, mergers and new issues. The top banks will regularly advise over a hundred large firms each. They will invariably be involved in all major take-over battles.

- *Fund management*: looking after the funds of pension funds, investment and unit trusts, etc. as well as central banks and private individuals. Management and advice cover both domestic and international investments. (See Chapter 5.)

- *Euro-currency and Euro-bond business*: most banks have involved themselves in underwriting sizeable issues and in the secondary

(*Continued on page* 20)

(Continued from page 19)

markets. (See Chapter 9.) Several have also become increasingly involved in markets in the sovereign debt of developing countries, known as LDC debt trading.

● Miscellaneous services: some traditional, some new, embracing property, shipping, timber, commodities, bullion, etc., etc.

As we shall see in Chapters 4 and 5, which explain the Stock Exchange and the capital market, the changes introduced by what has become known as 'Big Bang' in October 1986 radically affected the size and function of several of the leading merchant banks. With the deregulation of the London stock market, certain banks acquired stockbrokers, security houses or market makers and became international financial conglomerates capable of competing with the giant American and Japanese investment houses.

Which Banks do What

So far we have talked about banks in general. It is time to be more specific and to explain how they differ and what they all do. Banks can be divided up in several ways, but the following categories are the main ones:

1. The large *clearing or high street banks*, such as Barclays, Lloyds, Midland, National Westminster, Bank of Scotland, Royal Bank of Scotland, Trustee Savings Bank and Abbey National. They operate 14,500 branches in the UK.
2. *Merchant banks*, with such well known names as Barings, Hambros, Kleinworts, Lazards, Rothschilds, Schroders, Warburgs etc. The clearing banks have also created, or acquired, their own merchant bank subsidiaries.
3. *British overseas banks*, such as Standard Chartered and Grindlays (now part of the ANZ Banking Group). They have large numbers of branches in overseas territories.
4. *Foreign banks* operating in London through subsidiaries, branches or representative offices. There are now 526 in London.
5. *Nationwide retail banks* offering savings or money transfer services and other facilities, such as the National Savings Bank and the National Girobank.

In addition to the above essentially banking structure, there are the *building societies*, which are mutual organisations whose activities are

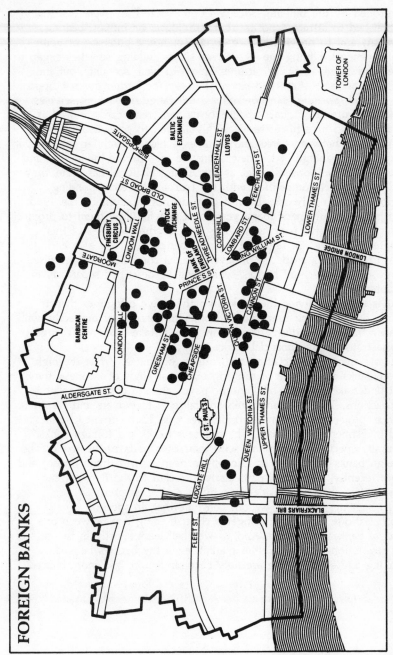

FOREIGN BANKS

● *Location of main foreign banks (source: Savills City Office Research Department)*

controlled by the Building Society Commission They were essentially established to attract deposits from individuals on interest-bearing accounts and to provide finance purely for house purchase or home improvements. During the 1970s and 1980s building societies began to offer current-account-type facilities linked to bank accounts, but the Building Societies Act 1986 paved the way for further diversification. As a result, Societies can now offer a full range of banking services, including current accounts, cheque cards and credit cards as well as insurance and investment services. This has led to considerable competition between banks and societies, which is likely to intensify. If they take advantage of the new ability to incorporate themselves and thus become authorised banks, as the Abbey National has done, they will be in direct competition with the banks, with corresponding regional branch networks. Even if they do not incorporate, the 1986 legislation, or any new liberal version of it, will allow them to provide several competitive banking services. But for the purposes of this chapter, we have not regarded them as banks. We have also excluded consortium banks, made up of several banks combined for specialised purposes, and discount houses, which will be described separately in Chapter 7.

It is easier to divide the banks into these five categories than to divide them by their functions. All of them, directly or indirectly, will finance trade and industry, lend money, undertake foreign exchange transactions or give financial advice.

Some are more specialised than others, of course. While the high street banks are capable of carrying out most kinds of business, they still undertake the bulk of domestic payments and consumer-related transactions. The merchant banks specialise in take-overs and corporate advice, project finance on a world-wide basis, Euro-currency business and investment transactions. The overseas banks and foreign banks naturally specialise in business with their own parts of the world. The foreign banks have been traditionally concerned with trade finance and, more recently, have been particularly attracted to the Euro-currency market. We shall be considering why in a later chapter.

To sum up, therefore, we can conclude that, in spite of specialisations, there is no longer a clear dividing line between one kind of bank and another. And, as we shall learn shortly in the case of the revolution in the securities market, even the barriers between banking and stockbroking are now becoming more and more blurred.

The Bank of England

The Bank of England remains at the centre of the City, physically and functionally. Its original Royal Charter, granted by King William and Queen Mary in 1694, indicated that it should 'promote the Public Good and Benefit our people'. The Bank now interprets this as maintaining the value of money, ensuring the soundness of the financial system and promoting the efficiency and competitiveness of financial markets.

What it Does

How does it do this? Over the centuries it has accumulated different responsibilities but the following are the main ones. At present the Bank of England:

- issues the country's bank notes;

- borrows on behalf of the Government by issuing Government securities;

- holds the Government's main bank account;

- holds accounts of clearing banks, discount houses, merchant banks, foreign banks, overseas central banks, the International Monetary Fund and a few industrial companies;

- advises on, and carries out, Government monetary policy, by its interventions in the money market, gilt-edged market and foreign exchange market;

- supervises the banking system, and other financial markets;

- maintains contact with other central banks and international financial institutions.

How it is Run

In 1694, when the Bank of England was established, its governing body, the Court of Directors, comprised a Governor, Deputy Governor and 24 directors. When it was nationalised (and another Royal Charter granted) in 1946, the number of directors was reduced to 16. All members of the Court are appointed by the Crown. The Court is required to meet once a week—traditionally on Thursdays.

(*Continued on page* 24)

There has been no doubt since 1946, how the Bank can be controlled from Whitehall. The Act establishing nationalisation put it firmly under Treasury control. Section 4(1) states that the Treasury may from time to time give to the Bank 'such directions... as, after consultation with the Governor of the Bank, they think necessary in the public interest'. However, this has never been implemented, so although ultimate power lies in Whitehall, the Bank has managed to retain discreet independence. The Governor meets the Chancellor regularly.

How it operates

In addition to the Governor and Deputy Governor, the Bank has four Executive Directors and a small number of Associate Directors with the same status. They have direct responsibility for the Bank's main financial operations:

- *Analysis, forecasting and information*   This covers forecasting and analysis of domestic financial and economic developments, as well as relations with the press and public.

- *International monitoring and analysis*   The Bank analyses international data and trends and maintains essential links with foreign central banks and other international institutions.

- *Wholesale markets supervision*   The Bank supervises the discount houses, gilt-edged market-makers and Stock Exchange money brokers as well as wholesale market intermediaries.

- *Managing the gilt-edged, money and foreign exchange markets*   This involves the management of monetary policy operations in the domestic markets and the currency markets, and the investment management of the UK reserves.

- *Banking and banking supervision*   The Bank is responsible for the note issue, the safe custody of bullion and securities and the Treasury bill issue as well as for the authorisation and supervision of deposit-taking institutions.

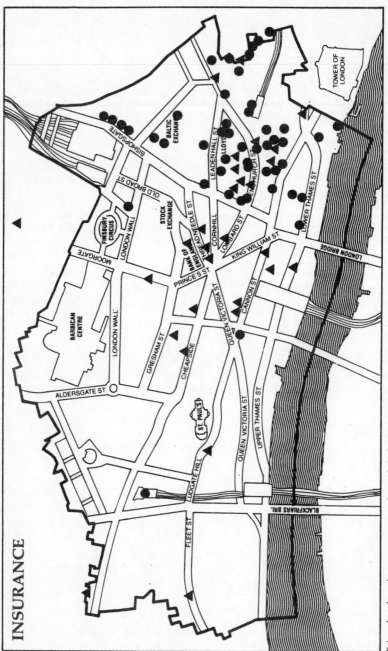

INSURANCE

Triangles show insurance companies and circles insurance brokers (source: Savills City Office Research Department)

3. Insurance

What is Insurance?

Insurance, one of the City's oldest activities, is about the sharing of risks. Whether it's the risk of losing your car, your house or your life or the risk of the destruction of a factory, supertanker or even an earth satellite, insurance provides a method of protection.

Insurance works on the principle that not everyone will suffer the same calamity at the same time; and that if we all make a contribution to a communal pool, there will be adequate funds to pay out the main sufferer in full. So by the payment of a sum of money, called the premium, we can be protected against certain specified risks.

Traces of maritime insurance in use in classical Greece and Rome give the industry as lengthy an ancestry as money lending. But, as in the case of banking, the real fundamentals of commercial insurance as we know it emerged much later: marine insurance in the eleventh or twelfth century: fire insurance in the seventeenth century: life assurance in the eighteenth and nineteenth centuries: and aviation and credit insurance in the twentieth century.

Although the terms 'assurance' and 'insurance' are now interchangeable, they originally had different meanings. 'Assurance' was taken out against a risk which was inevitable (e.g. death) or the reaching of a particular age, whereas 'insurance' was against a risk which might or might not happen.

How it Works

Thus the risks covered by insurance in its broadest sense are basically of two kinds: (i) events which are bound to happen, the date of which is either known or unknown; (ii) events which might or might not happen. In the first category come such things as term or endowment policies, under which money is paid out if a person dies or reaches an agreed age. In the second category are policies under which money is paid out if a car crashes, a house is damaged, or a ship sinks.

In each case the insurance process tends to be much the same. Individual contributions, known as premiums, are paid to the insurance company (or the insurer) by the insured, who receives a policy and is thus known as the policyholder. When (or if) the insured event takes place, a claim is made by the policyholder and a payment is then made out of the insurer's accumulated funds.

These funds are needed to meet such claims and are invested in a variety of ways, depending on the kind of insurance a company specialises in. Companies undertaking life insurance can match some of their investments to the expected pattern of their claims and can invest in longer-term securities.

Companies providing general insurance cover need to have investments which can be turned into cash, without undue loss or delay, and will have some of their money in shorter-term securities.

The Structure

So far we have been concerned with the way in which insurance developed and the principles on which it operates. We must now turn to the main operating participants in the London market. These are:

- Insurance and re-insurance companies
- Insurance brokers and intermediaries
- Lloyd's

We need to look at them separately, while bearing in mind throughout that one sector often overlaps with another. Some insurance companies (known as 'composite companies') undertake both life and non-life insurance business. Some brokers will provide business both to the companies and to Lloyd's. Some re-insurance companies will undertake general and life business and most insurance companies will undertake re-insurance business.

Insurance Companies

There are now some 839 insurance companies authorised to undertake insurance business in the United Kingdom. Of these 64 companies transact both life and non-life business (the 'composite' companies); 570 specialise in non-life business and 205 are specialist life companies. The big UK composite companies include such names as Commercial Union, Eagle Star, Guardian Royal Exchange, General Accident, Royal and Sun Alliance. Their main business, at home and abroad, will cover motor, fire, marine, aviation, transport, liability and personal accident classes.

Since some risks, including jumbo jets, industrial projects, oilfields, earthquakes and so on are so great, the process of spreading the risk has had to involve more and more companies. Specialised companies, called re-insurance companies, undertake such spreading of the big risks as their main function. Non-specialised companies as well as Lloyd's also undertake re-insurance. Some risks are so large that only the spreading of them i.e. the re-insuring of them, over hundreds of companies enables such risks to be covered The San Andreas fault in California and the nightmare of a major earthquake, with losses running into thousands of millions of dollars, is the kind of risk that re-insurance is meant to cope with. Collectively, insurance companies have an annual premium income of over £60,000 million.

Life Business

As their name implies, these companies concentrate on the provision of life insurance. They include companies, with shareholders, such as Prudential, Pearl and Legal and General, as well as mutual companies, basically owned by the policyholders, such as Norwich Union, Equitable Life and the Friends Provident.

The risks they cover can be put quite simply. One out of every four young men now aged 25 will not live to see his 65th birthday. On the other hand, the rest will do so and then need money to retire on. Either way, the man, and his family, will need help to prepare for either eventuality.

Until the middle of the eighteenth century, life insurance as we now know it (that is, based on a detailed analysis of life expectancy tables) did not exist. James Dodson worked out the first tables in 1756, averaging out what a person's annual premiums ought to be, based on patterns of mortality, the laws of averages and the arithmetic of compound interest. But he did not live to see his estimates converted into the life policies we now know. Now anyone can choose between:

- A *term policy*, which is a type of insurance policy that provides for an agreed sum of money to be paid to the policyholder's family or next of kin but only if the policyholder happens to die within an agreed period of time;
- A *whole life policy*, which provides for an agreed sum of money to be paid to the policyholder's family or next of kin when the policyholder dies, whenever that may be;
- An *endowment policy*, which provides a sum of money either at the end of an agreed period of time, or on the death of the policyholder, whichever of the two happens first; and
- An *annuity*, which is a form of life assurance that, like a pension, provides for a sum of money to be paid at regular intervals to the policyholder.

Lloyd's

Lloyd's is unique. It is not an insurance company. There is no equivalent of this remarkable insurance market to be found anywhere else in the world.

Since 1688, when Edward Lloyd first opened his coffee house in Tower Street for merchants to conduct their business, which often included underwriting of marine insurance risks, his successors (now known as the Corporation of Lloyd's) have fulfilled a similar function: the provision of a market place for insurance. Lloyd's, of course, is no longer an informal assembly of merchants meeting in a coffee house. Lloyd's today is a formally constituted society of underwriters whose members, known as 'names', all private individuals, accept insurance risks on a basis of unlimited personal liability.

There are more than 26,500 members of Lloyd's divided into some 354 syndicates, which vary in size. Each syndicate is managed by an underwriting agent who appoints a professional underwriter for each main class of business.

We shall be discussing the role of insurance brokers shortly, but in order to see how Lloyd's works, we need to begin with a Lloyd's broker bringing insurance business from a member of the public to Lloyd's. Let us assume it is a shipowner wishing to insure a new vessel.

The broker acting on behalf of the shipowner will immediately fill out a 'slip', setting out the details of the risk involved, and take it to the Underwriting Room at Lloyd's. He will then approach the underwriters, sitting in the narrow boxes, who deal in marine business, seeking the best 'quote' on behalf of the shipowner.

Once he has negotiated an acceptable rate, he gets the chosen underwriter to indicate on the slip what share of the total risk he is willing to accept. He is in effect 'leading' the underwriting, and the broker then proceeds to get similar agreements from other underwriters on the same basis. In this way the risk is spread among several underwriters.

We have spoken of the private wealth standing behind the risks taken on by Lloyd's members. Each member, or 'name', has to demonstrate an individual 'show of wealth' to the Committee of Lloyd's of at least £250,000. Names also have to lodge substantial funds at Lloyd's which establish the size of the business they can transact. Behind all this Lloyd's has a Central Fund, to protect the assured, of some £400 million. Yet the individual member's personal and unlimited liability is the element which makes Lloyd's so unique not only in London, but in the world.

The principle of unlimited liability has been subjected to some criticism recently as heavy trading losses have faced some Lloyd's names with the need to provide a large amount of additional financial support in order to be able to continue underwriting. New regulations have been introduced to extend the same degree of security to Lloyd's members as has always been given to Lloyd's policyholders. However, when all is said and done, Lloyd's members remain liable for normal trading losses to the full extent of their personal means, a requirement which is unlikely to change in the foreseeable future.

Lloyd's attracts business from throughout the world, and in 1991 had an annual premium income capacity of almost £11,400 million. The scope of the Lloyd's market now extends well beyond its original marine business to include aviation, space technology, road transport, offshore oil and gas exploration and such marginal oddities as a comedian's moustache, a film star's legs, and insurance to cover the payment of large prizes—say for the capture of the Loch Ness Monster or perhaps a professional golfer's hole-in-one.

Insurance Brokers

We have concentrated so far on how the insurance market works and what kind of a service the insurance market, made up of insurance companies and Lloyd's, offers the public. In the case of Lloyd's, we made the point that authorised brokers were an essential link between the public and the Lloyd's underwriter.

General insurance and life business, both outside Lloyd's, are sold in several different ways. The companies and the life offices have branches up and down the country through which policies are sold direct to the public. In addition, part-time agents, such as bank managers and solicitors, are often appointed by companies to channel business to them.

In addition there are the professional insurance brokers, who range from a small shop in the high street to a London-based international broker. They are full time specialists, offering detailed advice to clients, usually free of charge, receiving their income from a commission paid by the insurance companies (or Lloyd's underwriters). Such brokers offer independent advice not tied to one insurance company.

At one time, it was easy to set up as an insurance broker. But since 1981, a firm offering such services has to be registered and to meet the stringent requirements of the Insurance Brokers Registration Act. At present over 17,000 individual insurance brokers have been registered. Some 5,400 businesses are entitled to trade as insurance brokers.

Where Insurance Firms Invest their Money (1989)

Long-term funds
£275,870m

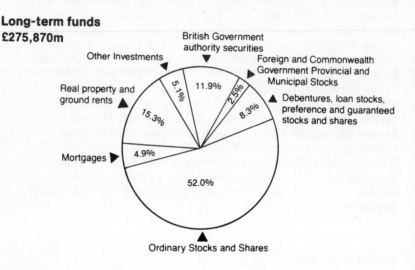

General funds
£46,580m

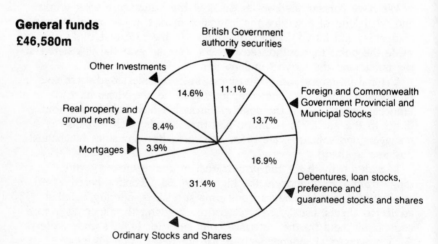

The insurance companies covered include British firms
and their overseas subsidiaries and British subsidiaries of
overseas companies. The investments are at market value.

Source: Association of British Insurers.

Foreign Business

Overseas business has been a significant part of the London insurance market for centuries. It remains so today. Over half of the total premiums flowing to Lloyd's and to the companies come from overseas.

This foreign business emerges in two ways—through the branches, agencies and subsidiaries of the companies in over 100 separate countries and through the insurance brokers who place the business with the companies or Lloyd's in London.

Something like a half of all the overseas business flowing to the London market comes from the United States, with 15 per cent coming from members of the Common Market.

The capacity of the London market is such that it can attract a larger share of the premiums arising from insurance business round the world than any other centre. It has enabled Lloyd's underwriters, for example, not only to pay out £150 million against claims when two earth satellites were lost in space, but also to finance their rescue by the space shuttle *Discovery*.

When such claims are deducted from the world-wide premiums, the London insurance market's net foreign income (i.e. its invisible income, which also includes portfolio income) comes out at £2,927 million.

Contribution to the Economy

We have now identified several ways in which the insurance companies and Lloyd's help the functioning of the economy and the smooth running, and expansion, of industry:

(i) By providing financial protection against loss from fire, theft, legal liability, pecuniary loss, interruption of production etc., insurance companies ensure that such calamities are immediately paid for, enabling finance to be devoted to the development of business.

(ii) By accumulating funds, out of premiums, to pay out future claims, insurance companies are able to invest large sums not only in Government securities but in industry itself. At the end of 1989, investments by insurance companies in British Government securities, debentures, loan stocks, preference and guaranteed stocks and shares and ordinary stocks and shares were £327,010 million. We shall be examining how this happens in Chapter 5.

(iii) The insurance industry is a major employer, with a workforce of 340,000.

(iv) Close to 80 per cent of all households have an involvement in the insurance industry through life insurance and virtually all households have one or more general insurance policies.

(v) After the payment of claims from its world-wide premiums, the London insurance market's net foreign income (its invisible income including portfolio income) comes out at £2,927 million.

4. The Stock Exchange

What It Does

The London Stock Exchange remains at the centre of the City and a stock market is at the heart of capitalism.

In essence, it is the place where investors with money to spare make contact with those in industry, commerce and Government who want to borrow it. In fact it is a market in stocks and shares, that is, where pieces of paper representing the ownership of companies or loans to Government and others can be bought and sold.

A capitalist society can flourish without a stock market. But it is only when one exists that the cost of finding new money for enterprises declines and money begins to flow freely into them.

The fear that an investor cannot freely sell his shares in a company immediately blocks new financing. And the knowledge that an investment in a company (through the acquisition of shares) can be sold wherever it is needed elsewhere is a major incentive to investors. A stock market provides such re-assurance.

What It Is

In 1986 the Stock Exchange merged with the International Securities Regulatory Organisation (ISRO) to form a self-regulatory organisation (SRO) and a recognised investment exchange (RIE) called the International Stock Exchange. Today the exchange is known simply as the London Stock Exchange. Member firms wishing to undertake investment business on the Exchange need to be registered with an SRO. The Securities and Futures Authority (SFA) sets the rules for securities houses dealing with clients and monitors their conduct accordingly. The Exchange meanwhile continues to act as a competent authority for the listing of securities.

Over 7,000 securities are traded on the London Stock Exchange. In 1990 the turnover in these securities was valued at over £1,666.6 billion. The largest single borrower of funds is the Government, which in return offers gilt-edged and fixed interest securities for sale to investors. In 1990 the volume of trading in such gilt-edged stocks accounted for 40 per cent of total Stock Exchange turnover.

How It Began

Seventeenth century London was one of the largest trading ports in Europe and a centre for all kinds of economic activity. As the rewards of trade with the newly discovered continents increased, so did the risks, and many merchants were happier to take a part or a *share* of the venture, in return for a slice of the potential profits.

However, voyages were long and most investors were not prepared to put up money in the first place, unless they could cash in their shares whenever they wanted. This demand for liquidity led to holders of shares meeting at known places, often coffee-houses, where shares could be exchanged, or sold, and where entrepreneurs could go to find funds to finance their projects. Such meetings were taking place as early as the 1770s.

Not until 1802 was the Stock Exchange formally constituted, when it was felt necessary that a controlled and recognised procedure should be established to enable investors to buy and sell shares without undue difficulty or risk, and thus make it easier for companies to raise funds to finance expansion. This experience was not unique to London either; Amsterdam was the first city to develop such an Exchange and a host of capitalist countries have each felt a need to establish their own Exchanges at a particular stage in their economic development.

How It Used to Work

The easiest way to appreciate the workings of the London market is to consider an individual transaction. Let us assume that you have just inherited some money from a relative. You are advised by a stockbroker to invest some of the money on the Stock Exchange. Before the changes which took place in 1986, the stockbroker would act solely as a 'middle man' between yourself, the client, and the wholesaler of shares known as the stockjobber.

The stockbroker had access to a lot of detailed information about the companies which are listed on the Exchange and would give you advice on which of these he recommended as a good investment. Having made your choice, aided by your stockbroker's professional opinion, he would then go onto the floor of the Exchange on your behalf and purchase the shares from a stockjobber. Members of the public were not allowed to buy shares from the jobbers directly. All transactions had to be carried out through the offices of a stockbroker. Once on the floor, the stockbroker would go round the various stalls, or jobbers' *'pitches'* as they were known, and ask the jobbers what was their price for the shares he wanted to buy. The broker would not say at that stage whether he was buying or selling, as the two prices (lower for buying, higher for selling) quoted to him by the jobbers would vary from pitch to pitch. Having worked out which jobber was selling at the cheapest, he could go back to him and arrange to purchase the shares on behalf of his client. Exactly the same process was gone through when a broker wished to sell shares on behalf of his client. It should be added that telephones and information screens also played their part in these transactions.

What we have described is the way in which the London market operated between 1912 and 1986. Under this arrangement, known as 'single-capacity' dealing, the broker and the jobber had separate functions: the jobber acting as a wholesaler and making his profit from the margin between his buying and selling prices and from his dealings in the shares, the broker charging a fixed commission to his client. The jobber, having quoted a price, was obliged to trade with the broker, just as the broker was obliged to get the best possible price for his client.

Reasons For Change

This system worked well and not only protected the investor from a smart dealer wanting to offload a block of doubtful shares, but ensured competitive prices from the jobbers, as well as smoothing out excessive price fluctuations.

On 27 October 1986, the Stock Exchange introduced major changes: the abolition of the fixed brokers' commission, the introduction of negotiated commissions and the end of 'single capacity' dealings. The changes which took place are commonly referred to as 'Big Bang'. Before these changes, preparations for 100 per cent ownership of dealing firms by other financial institutions had been completed. What we need to explore is why.

Several factors, some domestic, some international, had brought about this transformation. They were:

● The British Government's conviction that fixed commissions had been inhibiting competition in the London stock market.
● The dramatic rise in the volume of investing funds in the hands of big financial institutions, such as pension funds, insurance companies, unit and investment trusts, had put pressure on the fixed commission arrangements, and led to proposals for negotiated commissions.
● The financial cost of holding a growing volume of equity and fixed interest securities had strained the wholesale capacity of the

jobbers and highlighted the lack of capital funds under present arrangements.
- A growing amount of London-based international security business had been by-passing the London Stock Exchange (because of the fixed commissions) and was being undertaken by the London offices of overseas security houses.
- Shares in certain major UK companies, such as ICI, had been trading more heavily in New York than in London.
- The growing international use of technology in security markets for information, communication and even dealing.

These were the main elements leading to the changes in 1986.

The Changes

The process of change began on 27 July 1983, when the Chairman of the Stock Exchange agreed to abolish minimum commissions by the end of 1986. From this commitment emerged other structural changes.

The first was the proposal to change from 'single capacity' to 'dual capacity', under which a single firm can act both as agent and principal, acting on its own behalf as well as on behalf of its clients. This change in turn allowed (with the encouragement of the Stock Exchange and the Bank of England) individual firms to increase their capital resources and other financial institutions, such as banks, to buy stakes in such Member Firms. As a result banks had been able to buy 100 per cent of Member Firms since the spring of 1986, prior to the introduction of negotiated commissions in October 1986, having previously been allowed to purchase up to 29.9 per cent. A dramatic change in the structure of the securities industry thus took place, with UK clearing and merchant banks and foreign banks acquiring stakes in existing broking and jobbing firms.

All this came about because of the pressure of competition, imposed at home and experienced abroad. London brokers were under pressure at home to cut, or at least to negotiate lower, commissions automatically imposed on the big financial institutions. As they rightly argued, it made little sense to impose fixed commissions on the remarkably large transactions they were bringing to the Exchange, since a large transaction costs little more to handle than a small one.

At the same time, American brokers, by the use of depository receipts in New York (basically pieces of paper representing share holdings which did not attract London stamp duty) were attracting an increasing volume of big business in London industrial shares across the Atlantic. Technology also began to suggest the possibility of 24-hour dealings in the world's top shares, so that ICI for example, could be bought or sold in Tokyo, London and New York.

Who Owns Shares

Share ownership has been rising significantly over the past decade. The latest survey, carried out in March 1991 by the Treasury and the Stock Exchange, showed that there are currently over 11 million people in the UK (25 per cent of the adult population) who own shares. This compared with 19 per cent in 1987 and an estimated 7 per cent in 1979. Britain is now second only to the United States in the level of share ownership.

Several factors have been helping this trend:

● The tax incentives offered to *employee share schemes*. In 1979 there were only 30 such schemes. Now there are around 1,927, involving two and a quarter million employees, who own, or hold options over, shares with an original value of over £6.5 billion.

● The tax incentives offered to *share option schemes* since legislation was passed following the 1984 Budget.

● The Government's *privatisation programme* has boosted personal share ownership. By returning 13 major state-owned companies to the free enterprise sector (including British Gas, British Aerospace, Britoil, the Electricity industry, TSB, British Airways and British Telecom), individuals who had not previously considered stock market investment became shareholders for the first time.

● The introduction of *personal equity plans* (PEPs). Over 1.2 million plans were taken out in 1990/91 with over £3 billion invested.

Sources: London Stock Exchange; the Treasury

The New Operators

What emerged, therefore, on 27 October 1986 was a stock market made up of broker/dealers, some of whom also act as 'market-makers'. The latter are capable of acting on behalf of clients as agents, of taking positions in shares, of making markets in shares, of assuming distribution and of undertaking their own research. On the other hand, some dealers now confine themselves to offering a simple 'no frills' service, buying and selling shares on behalf of clients.

The process of buying and selling shares has naturally changed too. An investor, approaching a broker/dealer, wishing to buy 1,500 shares in ICI, now relies, not on the competition between jobbers, but rather on the competitive prices offered by the market-makers. At first these prices were displayed on information screens on the trading floor, but as time went by the floor of the Exchange became less essential than it used to be. The floor has now become redundant. Business is transacted entirely within and between broker–dealers' offices.

So at one end we have simple operators; at the other end large financial conglomerates, linking banks and securities houses, capable of competing with the giants of New York and Tokyo. These large groupings, backed by extensive capital resources, thus combine the functions of issuing houses, market-makers, brokers, investment managers, deposit takers, providers of short and medium credit facilities, as well as insurance services.

New safeguards

This emergence of new, enlarged financial supermarkets has brought anxieties as well as opportunities. There are the obvious dangers of conflicts of interest within the same firm. There is also the danger that clients may suffer from the ability of a firm to act as both agent and as principal.

In other words, a broker/dealer might be tempted to recommend shares to a client which he has acquired as a principal. He may also be tempted to use information acquired in one capacity in executing a different one. As the City jargon put it, the gaps in the 'Chinese walls' erected between one activity and another, could lead to rather too much temptation.

Safeguards have clearly been needed. To understand what form these new safeguards take, let us first of all see how the investor is still protected under dual capacity.

Going back to our original client with a sum of money to invest, we must remember that under the old system no matter which broker he chose to do business with, the broker's commission on the deal was fixed. Therefore, brokers could not undercut each other, and similarly when on the floor of the Exchange, all brokers were obliged to find the best deal they could for their client. This being so, the broker had nothing to gain by suggesting poorly performing shares to his client; as his commission was secure, he offered the best advice he could, and found shares at the best price.

Also under the old single-capacity system, we remember that jobbers were not allowed to deal with the public directly. They only bought or sold when a broker wished to sell or buy from them and in this way investors could never be sold poorly performing shares unwittingly, since the broker was always there to act as advisor and professional go-between, with the client on one side and the jobber on the other.

However, with the new dual-capacity dealings, one can easily see how, if a dealer in shares is left with a particularly poor portfolio, he can say to a prospective client, 'I recommend you to buy share X, and I just happen to have 5,000 of them which I will be pleased to sell you'.

Under the former system of single capacity this could never arise, as the broker would know that share X was a bad buy and would dissuade his client from investing in it. Similarly, it might be asked, what is to stop a dealer buying shares from a client at below the market price or selling him a particular share above the odds? Again, under single-capacity dealing, the broker was duty bound to get the best price.

With the introduction of dual capacity in 1986, therefore, additional safeguards were needed. Those at present introduced or under discussion vary from new technology to new kinds of self-regulation:

- The introduction of the Financial Services Act provided a statutory frame-work covering investor protection, ensuring all securities houses undertaking investment business on behalf of clients complied with the rules laid down in the Act.
- The Exchange's computerised system SEAQ (Stock Exchange Automated Quotations System) was introduced on 27 October 1986. The system was developed to accommodate the high levels of turnover expected in association with Big Bang. The dissemination of price information via SEAQ allowed trading to take place from members offices, and soon after Big Bang the trading floor became redundant. Through SEAQ, market price information has become more visible to investors and market practitioners than ever before.
- The Securities Association (now part of SFA) introduced a comprehensive set of conduct of business rules which govern the relationship between the client and member firm or securities house. The principles contained within these rules ensure that clients are made aware of the firm's terms of dealing and in turn that firms put the interests of clients ahead of their own at all times. All securities houses registered with SFA to undertake investment business on behalf of clients are therefore required to abide by these rules. (See Chapter 15.)

In addition the Stock Exchange has extensive systems for supervising and monitoring the dealings of firms in each of its markets and for enforcing compliance with the rules governing member firms' activities.

The Exchange has direct access to the information input by firms into the central Checking System and the central price display mechanisms, SEAQ and SEAQ International. This, coupled with the information provided to the Exchange's Company News Service, allows the Exchange to maintain a comprehensive database of detailed information which can be used to investigate any irregularities. In addition, the Exchange's Insider Dealing Group co-operates closely with the Department of Trade and Industry. The DTI is able to delegate authority to the Stock Exchange should prosecution cases arise.

The stringent rules enforced by the SFA regulating its membership, together with close scrutiny and monitoring of the Exchange's markets, should ensure investor confidence, thus rendering the London Stock Exchange a safe and secure market in which to trade.

These changes have enabled the London Stock Exchange to compete in world markets. It will also need to rely on exposure, disclosure, the clear separation of functions and strict regulation, if investors are to be protected from the potential abuses of dual capacity.

Impact of 'Big Bang' and 'Big Crash'

'Big Bang' took place overnight on 27 October 1986. A year later, on 19 October 1987, world stock markets suffered their biggest decline since 1929, the 'Big Crash'. The two events transformed the operations of the London security markets.

'Big Bang' opened up London to bigger, better capitalised dealing firms, allowing banks and brokers (domestic and foreign) to merge together and set up as market-makers. Competition intensified, turnover expanded and foreign security business was re-attracted to London.

The 'Big Crash' tested both the nerves of investors and the market's revised structure. It reduced turnover, heightened competition and led to significant losses by market-makers, running into hundreds of millions of pounds. The main results, and lessons, of the Crash were:

- Some of the new market-makers decided to cease trading in sectors of the market, some completely.
- The use of portfolio insurance to protect investments, which is extensively used in the United States, was shown to have major flaws if futures markets could not cope with heavy sales.
- Private investors did not desert the stock market and continued to trade.
- The London market remained open, in contrast to Hong Kong and, to a lesser extent, New York.
- Moves toward the global integration of securities markets (see Chapter 14) slowed down, but were not reversed.

5. The Capital Market

Money can be provided to an industrial firm in the form of a credit (see Chapter 2) or in the form of an issue of shares, debentures, bonds, etc. (see Chapter 4). The banks and the stock market are the dual providers. In one case money is lent to a borrower; in the other a financial instrument is bought and sold.

Some financial centres, for historical reasons, rely basically on bank finance; others on a combination of bank finance and stock market securities.

Active capital markets, like London and New York, can provide a variety of financial sources. The key to a successful one is the provision of new money and this in turn depends not only on flexible bank finance, but also on the existence of financial institutions capable of absorbing a growing volume of new securities. London's capital market is made up of:

(i) A stock market providing a *primary* market in new securities and a *secondary* market in existing securities.

(ii) Financial institutions, such as insurance companies, pension funds, investment trusts and unit trusts.

(iii) Specialised financial institutions, such as Investors In Industry, Equity Capital for Industry, Commonwealth Development Finance Company and the Agricultural Mortgage Corporation.

The size of funds available for investment through the main institutions (insurance companies, pension funds, investment trusts and unit trusts) can be judged from the following table:

Total assets (end March 1990)	(£ billions)
Insurance companies:	
Long-term funds	275.5
General funds	51.5
Pension funds	300.0
Investment trusts	20.6
Unit trusts	56.0

The way in which insurance companies and life offices accumulate their funds was explained in Chapter 3. We now need to look more closely into pension funds, investment trusts and unit trusts.

A. PENSION FUNDS

What They Are Pension funds arise out of the efforts to provide pensions (i.e. regular agreed payments) to employed people after they have retired. Some pension schemes, such as those relating to the central Civil Service, are financed direct from the Exchequer; that is, the ultimate pensions really come out of current tax revenue. But the bulk of occupational pension schemes are based on the pooling of regular payments into a trust fund, out of which future pensions will be paid.

A young person in his first job can, if he remains in employment, expect to be receiving wages or salaries for the next 45 or even 50 years and, thereafter, a pension for the rest of his life. His and his employers' contributions to the pension fund are thus piling up for a lengthy period before the retirement payments become due.

The pooling of the contributions, therefore, is the source for investments on the stock market and elsewhere. These investments have to match the pension funds' long-term obligations, that is their need to pay out retirement pensions up to 40 or even 45 years ahead.

How They Invest The way in which pension funds make investments vary, though the underlying obligations are clear. Pension funds are basically trust funds and as such the trustees are bound by legal restraints, imposed by their own trust deed and trust law. The trustees in turn will normally take investment advice from a bank, an insurance company or other professional investment adviser or, if the fund is big enough, from an in-house investment manager.

Their approach to investment is based on a number of factors: the age of the fund, the blend of ages of the employees, and their view of economic and financial trends, stretching decades ahead.

The age of the fund inevitably affects its rate of growth, since in the early years the income from contributions and from investments outstrips the outflow of retirement pensions. It normally takes some considerable time for a fund to reach a static position, that is, where its income and outgoings offset each other. Few British funds have yet reached this position, except in declining industries such as merchant shipping and coal.

Most factors point to the need for a long-term policy: the need to consider the future pension requirements of the latest recruit will itself stretch the investment horizon at least 60 years ahead. In a

---

Investment Management in the City

Investors, large and small, domestic and foreign, seek investment advice in the City. Until recently it was far from clear how many investments were under management or advice, and by whom. A recent Bank of England survey provided the following facts:

● London and Edinburgh have become major centres for both domestic and international fund management.

● No figures are available for total funds under management, but UK institutional investors had assets totalling over £700 billion at the end of 1989.

● A substantial proportion of funds from other European countries, as well as the European specialist sectors of major US and Japanese funds, are managed from the UK.

● In 1988 US pension fund foreign assets totalling $16 billion were managed in the UK.

● The *main institutions* undertaking such management and advice were merchant banks, clearing banks, stockbrokers, insurance companies, unit trusts and investment trusts.

● The *main clients* for such advice are the pension funds, accounting for nearly 60 per cent of the domestic total, followed by unit trusts and investment trusts.

● The *big funds* are mainly managed by the merchant banks.

---

normal, still growing scheme, the investment advisers will be looking 40 or more years ahead.

How will this affect their choice of investments? A few general points will illustrate how they tend to go about it:

(i) They will want to ensure a guaranteed income flow for a longish period. This may point to the acquisition of long-dated Government securities.

(ii) They will want to ensure capital growth in the fund's assets. This may suggest investments in industrial ordinary shares (equities).

The Largest UK Pension Funds

Market Value of Investments, 1990

	£ billions
British Coal	12.6
British Telecom	11.8
Electricity Council	8.5
Post Office	7.7
British Rail	6.8
British Gas	5.2
Barclays Bank	5.2
Universities Superannuation Scheme	4.9
Shell Pensions Trust	4.8
British Petroleum	4.7
British Steel	4.2
ICI	4.1
National Westminster Bank	4.0
British Airways	3.3
Lloyds Bank	3.0
Midland Bank	2.6
Unilever	2.2
Strathclyde Regional Council	2.2

(*Source*: National Association of Pension Funds Year Book 1991)

(iii) They will be aware of the dangers of future inflation. This too may tempt them to consider ordinary shares, index-linked Government bonds and property.

(iv) They will be aware that longer-term obligations enable them to await certain investment developments. They can, therefore, consider investing in large-scale property developments, where income is delayed.

(v) They will be aware of having future obligations in sterling, but conscious of obtaining a better chance of growth in equity markets overseas. Often this may suggest a target of around 15 per cent in foreign equities.

These are just a few of the factors to be considered in deciding on the final blend of their investments. Their decisions will then make up part of the total institutional investments on the stock market and elsewhere. The pension funds have become a powerful influence on the capital market over the past decade and a half. There are now over 90,000 occupational pension schemes in the country. While 79,000 have fewer than 30 members, at least 44 have assets of over £1 billion. Two have assets of over £10 billion. Their total assets are now some £300 billion.

B. INVESTMENT TRUSTS

Spreading risks seems to be a City habit. It is, as we have already seen, the basis of insurance. It is also the investment approach taken by both investment trusts and unit trusts.

Both kinds of trusts approach the investment issue (and its solution) differently: but both work on the principle of *not* having all your eggs in the same basket. They provide a method whereby a non-professional investor can invest small amounts of money in a variety of shares. The easiest way to understand how they do this is to explain how each works and then to compare one with the other.

How Investment Trusts Started   Investment trusts were on the scene first, roughly half a century before unit trusts. The Foreign and Colonial Government Trust, formed in 1868 and quoted on the Stock Exchange just over ten years later, invested in a selection of eighteen overseas government stocks. The aim then, and now, was to give the investor of moderate means the same advantage as the large investor in reducing his risk by spreading the investment over a number of different stocks, so that the risk would be spread and the individual investor would not be in the position of losing all his savings if one of the shares chosen suddenly collapsed. Even the spreading of risks did not save some of the early participants, especially during the so-called Baring Crisis of 1890. But other investment trusts, including the Foreign and Colonial Government Trust, survived and lessons were learnt.

Buying Investment Trust Shares   Until quite recently, the only way to buy shares in an investment trust was through a stockbroker or dealer, as for any other shares. Since 1984, however, managers of investment trusts have been introducing savings schemes and investment schemes, which are a way to buy shares directly through the managers, often at less cost than going to a dealer in shares.

How They Work   An investment trust is a company, quoted on the Stock Exchange, which invests shareholders' funds, not in machinery to make things, but in shares in other companies. The choice of shares is made by professional investment trust managers. The income from the shares chosen is largely distributed to its own shareholders by way of dividend and partly used to cover its running costs and to build up

47

reserves for lean years. Most investment trusts aim at high capital appreciation for their stockholders, reflected in the price of the shares and underlying asset values.

This process gives the investment trust several features:

(i) It spreads the investment risks over several shares.
(ii) It can provide exposure to overseas markets, special situations, unlisted securities etc.
(iii) It provides professional investment expertise.
(iv) Dividend income is distributed regularly among the investment trust's shareholders and the price of the investment trust share in the stock market, together with its asset value, reflects some of the success (or failure) of the investment policy used.

How 'Gearing' Works One additional investment trust feature arises from the relationship between a trust's ordinary shareholders and its ability to borrow further funds to purchase additional shares. This kind of borrowing is a form of 'gearing' (or 'leverage' in the United States). In simple terms, such borrowing, through a term loan, for example, enables a trust to buy more shares. If the stock market rises, there is capital appreciation, which enables the trust to service the loan. If share prices fall, the reverse happens.

On this basis, the ordinary shareholder will receive a dividend related to the success or failure of the investments (after the term loan interest has been paid). Now when the stock market is rising and an investment trust's investments are sharing in its buoyancy, a trust's ordinary shareholders will be receiving a higher proportion of its total income than their nominal share and the reverse will be true when the stock market is falling. This so-called 'gearing' means that the whole of the growth in income, over and above the servicing of the loan, accrues to the ordinary shareholder. It explains why shares of investment trusts with high gearing (i.e. a high proportion of borrowing) will rise faster than the Stock Exchange average when share prices are rising and will fall faster than the average when the stock market is falling. Borrowing can also take place abroad, but in this case the trust has also to contend with fluctuations in the value of a loan expressed in foreign currency.

You may wonder what happens when stock markets fall, as they occasionally do. Fortunately, there are ways of protecting shareholders from the *adverse* effects of 'gearing'. One of the most common is for the investment manager to 'go liquid', that is, to arrange to sell certain shares and hold the money in cash. Secondly, he can invest a proportion of his total fund in loan capital or preference shares. Thirdly, he could consider buying back the trust's own loan capital. Each method has the effect of protecting the trust's ordinary shareholder from a bigger than normal drop in his income. The difficulty, of course, lies in guessing when such protection is needed.

Why There is a Discount   The fixed capital of an investment trust can be switched from one share to another. This flexibility is helped by the Inland Revenue agreement not to charge them capital gains tax on any gains. Such gains are not distributed in cash, but are used to build up the investment trust's portfolio. Basically a trust's assets are increased, when it invests successfully.

The valuation of a trust's assets thus becomes a major measuring rod of a trust's success. Net asset values (that is gross assets less liabilities) can then be compared with a trust's share valuation. If a trust's net assets are divided by the number of a trust's ordinary shares, the result is what is known as 'net asset per share' and can be compared with the share price of the trust in the stock market. If the share price is above the net asset value per share, it is said to stand at a *premium*; if below, it is said to be at a *discount*. In recent years investment trust shares have been standing at a discount, sometimes as high as 40 per cent; more recently nearer 20 per cent.

What accounts for the discount? The answer is a combination of factors. To some extent it reflects the cost of breaking up an investment trust to get at the basic shares; to some extent it reflects the competition from other, more publicised, investment vehicles, such as unit trusts; and to some extent it reflects the share performance of individual trusts. Whatever the reason, the discount means that such an investment is costing the shareholder in an investment trust less than if he invested directly in the underlying shares.

The original aim of the first investment trusts, apart from spreading risks, was to secure a high income for its shareholders. Some still concentrate on income. But specialisation now has spread to other targets, such as capital growth or overseas investment, or individual industries. The choice is remarkable. There are now over 240 investment trusts, managing some £21 billion of investors' funds with the spread of specialisation covering most geographical areas and industry sectors.

C. UNIT TRUSTS

How Unit Trusts Started   Unit trusts are more recent arrivals on the City scene. They can be said to have begun in 1931 when a London stockbroker brought the idea with him from a visit to the United States. As a result Municipal and General launched the First British Fixed Trust on 22 April 1931.

The original idea was that investors' money would be invested in a *fixed* number of chosen shares, which would be held for an agreed number of years. This would ensure a spreading of the risks and a higher yield than was obtainable on $2\frac{1}{2}$ per cent Consols. The experiment was successful, various flexibilities were introduced and by 1939 there were no less than 89 such unit trusts, operated by 15 management companies, with some £80 million under investment.

How They Work   The best way to understand how unit trusts work is to compare them with the investment trusts we have just been considering. The basic difference is that, whereas supply and demand for investment trust shares affect the share price of the trust itself, demand for unit trusts simply affects the size of the fund. The price of unit trusts, which is usually calculated daily, depends on the value of the underlying assets. Unit trusts are thus said to be 'open-ended'; that is, they can grow or shrink and their size depends entirely on the purchase or sale of units by investors.

Let's take this step by step. Money invested in a unit trust is pooled in a trust fund which invests the money in stocks and shares, according to the terms of its trust deed. This deed is usually drawn up by the managers of the fund and the trustee, and authorised by the Securities and Investment Board (see Chapter 15). The trustee is there to safeguard the fund; the management to undertake the investments and the sales of the units. A leading bank or insurance company normally acts as trustee. Thus the investor buys or sells 'units' and the money is added to or subtracted from the trust fund.

Unit trust prices are quoted in the newspapers showing a higher and a lower figure. The lower figure is called the 'bid' price and is the figure at which the managers are ready to buy back units from existing investors; the higher figure is the 'offer' price at which they are prepared to sell new or existing units. The offer price includes the cost of buying the underlying securities together with the managers' initial charge, which is calculated by a formula laid down by the Securities and Investment Board.

Unit trusts have come a long way since they were introduced into the UK in 1931. They have become much more flexible and specialised in the way they are managed and organised. They now offer a vehicle for the small and professional investor alike. They offer the advantage of a spread of risks, professional management and access to funds on demand. Unit trusts also offer savings plans as well as a combined unit-linked package with the life assurance industry. And, through various offshore financial centres, they offer a variety of so-called

How Unit Trusts and Investment Trusts Compare

Unit Trust	*Investment Trust*
Investors' money buys units in trust fund. The fund buys or sells underlying securities (mainly quoted stocks and shares).	Investors' money buys shares in investment trust company. Capital is used to buy or sell underlying securities.
Units bought from unit trust managements.	Investment trust shares bought on stock market or from managers through a savings scheme.
Number of units can be increased or decreased.	Share capital is fixed.
Offer price is fixed by managers and relates to value of underlying assets and includes some management costs.	Share price is quoted on stock market. No management costs are included.
Cannot borrow additional funds.	Able to borrow additional funds (to achieve 'gearing').
Sale of units can be advertised.	Sale of shares cannot be advertised.

'offshore units' (although these funds operate to different rules and are not covered by the compensation schemes).

At present approximately 1400 different unit trusts are available and total investments at the last count had reached over £56,000 million.

6. The Gilt-edged Market

What it is

As we noticed in Chapter 4, turnover in Government securities forms a substantial proportion of Stock Exchange business. The market in Government securities, otherwise known as the gilt-edged market (from the high-quality gilt-edged paper of the early certificates) is significant for other reasons too. At a time of high Government borrowing from the public, it becomes intertwined both with the Budget (fiscal policy) and interest rates (monetary policy). It deserves a chapter on its own.

How it began

The present gilt-edged market is closely connected with the Bank of England and the Stock Exchange. One controls it; the other used to house it. And it is not surprising to find that all three were just as closely intertwined at the beginning.

Kings and governments have needed to borrow throughout history. After centuries of such borrowings (and defaults) by kings of England and their governments, a more formal arrangement was agreed in 1694, when the British Government borrowed a further £1,200,000 to support the war against France, in return for the incorporation of the Bank of England, with the right to issue notes up to the value of its capital. Just over a century later, as we noted earlier, the Stock Exchange was formally established and, within a year, issued its first regular official list of prices. Gilt-edged stocks (though not described as such until 1892) were prominent in the list.

The Bank of England thus became the Government's agent in raising official loans and eventually the Stock Exchange became the obvious market place for their sale and purchase. For most of the eighteenth century, Government securities were sold to companies such as the East India Company and rich friends of ministers. Then, towards the end of the eighteenth century, Government stock was extended to the public generally.

Why it is Needed

The Bank of England still plays the same role today. It issues new longer-term Government securities to the public or to the market; it issues shorter-term, 3 month Treasury bills to the financial institutions; it holds the Government's main Exchequer accounts into which all taxes and the proceeds of all official borrowings flow; and it keeps a record of all Government stockholders, makes all interest payments and arranges the final repayment or conversion (into other longer-dated stocks) of existing securities.

The Government issues its own securities to the public for a simple reason. In spending money on roads, schools, housing, hospitals, defence, etc., a Government will often incur expenditure beyond the inflow of taxes. Sometimes this will be seasonal, since tax bills fall due at certain times of the year. Sometimes it will be deliberate, in an attempt to stimulate the economy. Whatever the reason, the Government will need to borrow money from the public. And the Bank of England, as its agent, will arrange the issue of Government securities, ranging from three-months' Treasury bills to gilt-edged stocks with a maturity of thirty years or more. In undertaking this task between 1786 and 1986 the Bank used the senior partner of Mullens & Co. as the Government Broker. Since 'Big Bang' the Government Broker has been a senior official of the Bank of England.

What Gilts Are

The market on which such Government securities are bought and sold is now run by 19 gilt-edged market-makers. If you or I wish to buy Government securities, we have a choice. We can buy securities which have no final repayment date, referred to as 'undated'. In this case the price simply moves up and down in relation to current rates of interest. We can buy securities with repayment dates up to five years ahead known as 'shorts'; from five to fifteen years ('medium'); or over fifteen ('longs'). More recently Government securities have been issued which are index-linked, that is, they allow for annual inflation and are directly linked to the retail price index.

Gilt-edged stocks have several characteristics. The main ones are that they are fixed-interest debt instruments; the interest payments and eventual redemption (where appropriate) are obligations of Government; they usually have a redemption date (that is a date on which full repayment is made); and they have an interest rate 'coupon', that is, the amount of interest to be paid each year (usually half-yearly) on the nominal value of the stock. Since the coupon rate per £100 of nominal stock is fixed when the stock is issued, change in the stock's market price leads to a corresponding change in its yield. For example, if £100 nominal of a 10 per cent stock is bought at a market price of £200, the running yield to the purchaser will be 5 per cent on the sum invested. Because of this connection, changes in the level of interest rates will be reflected in changes in the price of Government securities.

At present, gilt-edged stocks offer several advantages to the purchaser. The brokers' commission is much lower than on industrial shares. They do not attract the Government's stamp duty (although its imposition on equities will disappear soon). And they do not become liable for capital gains tax.

How Gilts Are Issued

The way in which new Government securities are issued to the public is unique to London. Stock can be issued immediately or over a period. For example, an issue of say £500 million $3\frac{1}{2}$ per cent Treasury stock will be announced at a certain minimum price. The price chosen is judged according to other gilt-edged prices. Thereafter bids are invited.

Amount of Gilt-Edged Stocks			
(£ millions: nominal value)			
End February:	1988	1989	1990
British Government Securities:			
Stocks	139,488	135,588	120,268
Of which index-linked	12,662	13,016	12,548
Bearer bonds	74	60	51
	139,562	135,648	120,319
Other Securities:			
Government-guaranteed	10	10	240
Commonwealth and overseas	2,442	2,625	3,144
Local authorities	117	112	106
Other	347	327	224
	2,916	3,074	3,714
Total	142,478	138,722	124,033

Source: Bank of England Report and Accounts, 1990

If the price is tempting, the whole issue may be absorbed at once. If not, the amount not immediately taken up by the market will later be sold on demand to the market. It becomes known as a 'tap' stock, i.e. it is available 'on tap' when needed until supplies are exhausted. Some issues (or new tranches of existing securities) are now sold 'on tap' from the outset. More recently, index-linked Government stocks have been issued by tender, without a minimum price specified in advance. The holding of an auction in short-dated gilt-edged stock has also become an established feature. The total value of Government stock outstanding at present is some £124 billion.

How the Market Works

The structure of the market changed radically after 'Big Bang'. In line with the changes introduced in the stock market generally, the gilt-edged market was also transformed. The introduction of dual capacity meant an end to the operations of the jobbing firms and the introduction of several new operators. The market now consists of four different participants:

● *Market-makers.* These are primary dealers, obliged to make an effective two-way market in gilts at all times and to accept Bank of England supervision. They deal direct with the big financial institutions by telephone.

● *Inter-dealer brokers.* They provide dealing facilities between the market-makers.

● *Stock Exchange money brokers.* They provide stock borrowing and lending facilities to the market-makers.

● *Broker dealers.* They provide agency facilities for investors, but also deal as principals if they so wish.

The gilt-edged market is still part of the Stock Exchange and the participants are members of the Stock Exchange and thus subject to its regulations, as well as being supervised by the Bank of England.

As in the case of the Stock Exchange generally, the gilt-edged market uses information screens, especially between the market-makers and the inter-dealer brokers who provide dealing facilities between them. Dissemination of prices by telephone or on screens has thus shifted business 'upstairs', off the floor of the Stock Exchange itself.

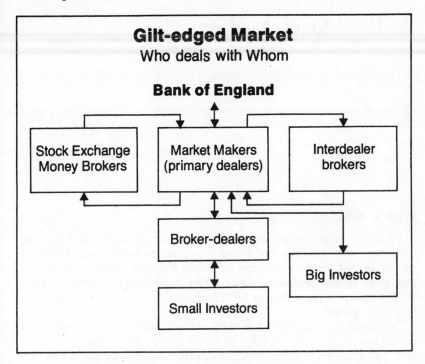

Gilt-edged Market
Who deals with Whom

Bank of England

| Stock Exchange Money Brokers | Market Makers (primary dealers) | Interdealer brokers |

Broker-dealers

Big Investors

Small Investors

The new technology has also extended to the Bank of England's *Central Gilts Office*, which offers a computerised service of payments and settlements between members. This eliminates the need for paper transfers, certificates and cheques; it reduces settlement risks; and it is easy to use, enabling members to see their up-to-date stock positions at the touch of a button.

Thus the present gilt-edged market is now similar to the American pattern of primary dealers. Two basic differences remain, however. The Bank of England has become part of the market with its own dealing room in the Bank. Secondly, London has maintained the existing distinction between dealers in gilt-edged stocks and the discount houses, who operate in the money market.

The methods of selling new securities are likely to evolve further. So called 'tap stocks', through the market-makers, will no doubt continue although the pool of new capital brought into the market by the bigger units may encourage experiments as the market develops.

7. The Money Market

What it does

When we were considering how banks make use of the deposits left with them, we said they had found it prudent to keep some of the money in cash or on short-term loan to the money market, just in case some of the depositors wanted their money back in a hurry. The short-term loans were said to be 'liquid', that is they could be turned into cash quickly.

This leads us straight to the heart of the London money market and to the role it plays in the City. Its function is a simple one: to borrow and lend spare money for short periods. It is hardly the place you or I would invest the odd £50. But it is the equivalent of a savings deposit account for the big financial institutions, large industrial corporations, local authorities, even governments. And, hardly surprisingly, the British Government has found it useful for its own monetary purposes.

The market as a whole attracts spare cash in large lumps and, through those who, like the discount houses, make a market in money or near-money instruments, invests it in such assets as Treasury bills, commercial bills, certificates of deposit and short-term Government securities. It is in essence a wholesale market in money.

We have spoken so far of *a* money market. There are in fact two separate, though closely related, money markets in the City: (i) the traditional market in short-term securities, such as bank acceptances and certificates of deposit, centred on the discount houses, who predominantly finance themselves with borrowings *secured* on their assets; and (ii) the interbank market, or parallel money market, concerned with *unsecured* lending. The basic difference is that in the case of a secured loan, the lender is given some protection, in the form of a security, by the borrower.

58

How they operate

(i) Discount Market. This market centres on nine discount houses who buy bills of exchange and other short-term securities created by the commercial banks and sell them to banks and other investors needing liquid assets. This stock-in-trade is largely financed by short-term borrowing from the banking system.

The discount houses play the important role of a monetary buffer between the banks and the Bank of England, channelling cash from the banks to other borrowers, both Government and commercial, through the purchase of bills, and short-term Government securities. This helps the banks to find a home for their spare cash, even overnight, and at the same time enables other borrowers to find short-term funds.

The discount houses, or bill brokers, have been playing this role for something like a century and a half. Throughout this period the so-called bill of exchange has been the main borrowing instrument used. It is in effect evidence of a debt owed by one party to another, in respect of a trading transaction, and with an agreed date of payment, perhaps three months ahead. If the bill is simply drawn by one industrial firm and 'accepted' by another—its trading counterpart—it will be called a 'trade bill', but normally bills are accepted by a bank (an 'accepting house') who undertakes to become principally liable for payment at the bill's maturity. They then become known as 'bank bills'.

Originally the bill of exchange was used to finance the bulk of domestic trade by the large numbers of country banks. The bill brokers, the forerunners of the discount houses, made a market in these inland bills. As foreign trade developed, financed through London, the same mechanism was used and the international 'bill on London' came into prominence.

It was at this stage that the merchant banks (or accepting houses) began to accept a growing volume of these bills, making them particularly attractive to the discount houses, who were keen to buy them below their ultimate repayment price (i.e. at a discount, which would depend on the prevailing rate of interest). The discount houses would 'endorse' such bills, that is add their names, and therefore their guarantee, to the bills. Over the years other borrowing instruments were introduced too, especially Treasury bills and short-term Government securities, by which the Government borrows money from the financial institutions.

We can now try to sum up what the discount houses, through the discount market or traditional money market, now do:

● They act as 'principals' (i.e. in their own right), not as brokers.

● They buy and sell bank acceptances, Treasury bills, certificates of deposit etc. In other words, they 'make a market' in these securities.

● They finance their stock of these instruments by using them as collateral for secured borrowing from banks and others, thereby providing the banking system with a source of liquidity.

● They have a special relationship with the Bank of England (which we shall explain in a moment).

(ii) Inter-Bank Market. This is a less traditional market made up of banks, and, more recently, of other institutions such as commercial firms, local authorities, building societies and other financial institutions. Short-term funds are lent between institutions either direct or through brokers, on an 'unsecured' basis, i.e. not backed up with securities as collateral.

Although one sector of the market spills over into another, it is also a series of specialised markets. The specialisations cover lending to banks, local authorities, finance houses etc. The markets operate through the placing and taking of short-term deposits and the purchase and sale of certificates of deposit, in sterling and foreign currencies.

The bulk of the business consists of *inter-bank transactions* and the market has now become the main means for the transformation of retail deposits into wholesale funds for bank lending of all kinds. It is also the basis of the Euro-dollar market, since it attracts foreign currency deposits as well as sterling.

The *local authority market* is also well developed, and consists of short-term local authority loans extending from overnight to 364 days as well as local authority bills for up to six months. Local authority securities from one to five years are also available. Banks and other financial institutions are the main lenders in this market. Other borrowers in the money market include finance houses and building societies.

One of the major innovations in the money markets was the introduction in the mid-1960s of *certificates of deposit*. Dollar certificates were begun in 1966 and sterling certificates in 1968. Certificates of deposit are issued by banks and are negotiable instruments certifying that a certain sum will be repaid on a stated maturity date with interest. They are in effect certificates for bank deposits and have the advantage that they can be bought and sold and thus give the depositor an added assurance that he can re-obtain his money at an earlier date than originally agreed by selling in the market. This enabled longer-term deposits to be arranged.

Transactions in this market either take place directly between borrower and lender, buyer and seller, or through a small number of brokers who, like their counterparts in the foreign exchange market, with whom most of them are related, act through telephone and electronic information screens. Some of the broking firms are foreign exchange brokers and some stockbroking firms.

To sum up, the parallel money markets have the following characteristics:

- They link the major borrowers and lenders in short-term money together through money brokers.

- Their loans are unsecured.

- The Bank of England does *not* intervene directly in them.

- They provide the banks with a flexible source for funding their loans.

- They provide the mechanism for the transformation of maturities in the Euro-currency market.

Who Use the Markets?

We have already indicated the variety of institutions which make use of the money markets, both the traditional market and the parallel markets. They range from industrial and commercial firms to the leading financial institutions (banks, building societies, finance houses, etc.) and from local authorities to central Government.

The financial services to the City itself are self-evident (and we shall be explaining the impact of the discount market on interest rates and monetary policy shortly). What are not so obvious are the services to industry.

The market's bill discounting facilities are familiar, stretching back into the nineteenth century. They can be highly competitive with the more normal lending techniques of overdrafts or fixed-term loans. But lending is not the only facility available to industry and commerce. Borrowing, especially for short periods, can be equally rewarding.

Commercial money can be left in the money market for varying periods and remain both secure and liquid. A variety of instruments and facilities are on offer. Cash can be deposited overnight, at call (that is available at 24 hours' notice) or for any fixed maturity the lender specifies. On substantial sums, a rate close to the inter-bank rate will normally be paid.

A growing number of industrial firms now have regular telephone links with discount houses and money brokers and have already become part of the City's regular money business.

The Financial System

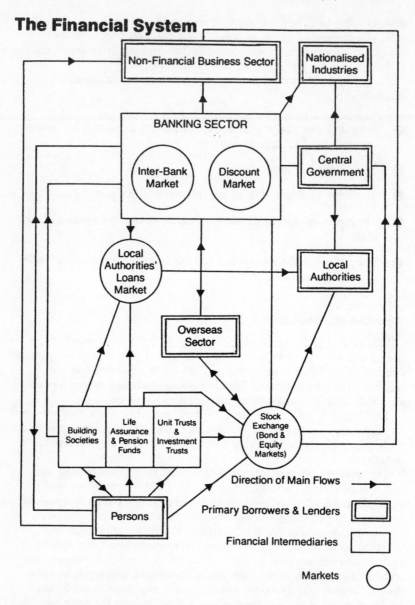

This diagram, prepared by Barclays Bank for its own *Barclays Review,* has been adapted to summarise (i) how one sector of the City relates to another, and (ii) how money flows to and from City markets to the general public and other parts of the economy.

How Monetary Policy Works

We have mentioned several times that the Government uses the traditional money market (that is, the secured market) to transmit its influence on monetary policy to the rest of the economy. It is time to explain how.

Although the mechanism has been tampered with several times in recent years, the key to the transmission process lies with the Bank of England. It plays two crucial roles: it acts as banker to the Government; it also acts as banker to the banks. It is, therefore, directly, involved in day-to-day transactions between the Government and the banks. Large sums of money flow from one to the other, through the Bank of England's accounts. The Bank can affect these flows through its operations in the traditional money market.

This is not the place to explain monetary policy or even monetarism in any great detail. Suffice to say that when British Governments believe that inflation or economic activity can be influenced by changes in the amount of money in circulation, or in the level of interest rates, they naturally turn to the money market as the place to take action. And they use the Bank of England as their main instrument.

In influencing the money market, the Bank of England has established a few helpful ground rules. These are:

● The Bank will aim to balance the supply of money in the market with the demand for it.

● It will do so, as far as possible, by operations in bills—Treasury bills, local authority bills, and commercial bills accepted by 'eligible' banks—carried out with the specialist market-makers, the discount houses.

● The discount houses must bid competitively for the money or bills which the Bank is making available, and the Bank will respond to bids for such amounts as will balance supply and demand unless it finds the rate unacceptable.

We are now in a position to see exactly how the Bank of England begins to influence policy.

The Bank publishes each morning at about 9.45 a.m., and if necessary revises at noon and 2 p.m., its estimate of the shortage or surplus of funds in the market that day. The estimate incorporates all the information available to the Bank about the prospective flows of money through the system, of which those between the Government and the banks are of particular importance. The publication of the estimate helps the banks to decide how much money they can place with the discount market, or need to draw from it by calling deposits, or whether to sell bills to or buy bills from the market. Most of these transactions are undertaken before noon, by which time the shortage or surplus of the day should be accurately mirrored in the positions of the discount houses.

The Bank usually undertakes bill transactions with the discount houses at 12.15 p.m. and at 2.15 p.m. (on days of exceptionally large shortage it may do an 'early round' at 10 a.m.). It will deal in Treasury bills, local authority bills or 'eligible' bank bills—bills accepted by one of those institutions on the Bank's list of 'eligible' names, and having no more than 91 days to go to maturity.

It is in its response to the offerings by the houses that the Bank exercises its influence on monetary conditions and interest rates. It will see what level of rates would result from dealing in the quantity needed to balance the supply and demand for cash.

If it finds those rates acceptable, it will deal accordingly. If it finds the rates on bills offered for sale to the Bank too low, it will decline those offers, so failing to relieve the shortage fully and driving market interest rates up. If it finds rates too high, it could accept additional amounts at somewhat lower rates and, by providing more cash than is needed, drive rates down. The Bank can also lend direct to the discount houses.

Out of these transactions emerges a pattern of short-term interest rates in bills as well as a reasonably clear signal about official hopes and intentions. The banks react accordingly and make their own individual decisions about what is known as *base rate*. This is the rate of interest on which their own lending (on overdraft or loan) is based. And it, in turn, affects building society mortgage rates and other interest rates elsewhere.

Base rate is, in that way, playing the role of the old official *Bank rate* or the more recent *minimum lending rate* (MLR). But, it must be noted, the Bank has not entirely replaced MLR. If it wishes to signal a significant rise in interest rates it can still do so by the use of MLR, that is, by announcing the rate at which it is prepared to lend money to the market.

One example of the way in which MLR can be used when the markets are closed, and when the Bank is thus unable to deal, occurred on the entry of sterling into the Exchange Rate Mechanism of the European Monetary System in the autumn of 1990. The Bank of England announced a full one-point cut in MLR at 4 p.m. one Friday afternoon, to operate from the following Monday. So MLR remains in reserve, in addition to the Bank's ability to deal in the money markets, as an instrument of monetary policy.

8. Foreign Exchange

Need for Foreign Currency

You take a holiday in France. I buy shares in a Japanese company. A friend sells equipment to an importer in Pittsburg. The Government lends money to Bangladesh. In each case and at some time, these different actions will lead to a need to exchange pounds into a foreign currency or the other way round. So we must now explore how the City helps these transactions to take place.

Several practical questions arise at the outset. Where do the French francs come from? How does the supplier of Japanese shares get paid? Where does the American importer get hold of the pounds to pay for the equipment? Who helps the Government to transfer monetary aid to Bangladesh?

These are the first questions, and we shall do our best to answer them as we go along. But they lead immediately to several more fundamental ones. Which parts of the City are involved in obtaining the foreign currency? Where do they do it? Who decides how many French francs, American dollars or Japanese yen we get for our pounds?

The short answer is the foreign exchange market. In the time-span of only one generation, the London market has been transformed from a leisurely top-hatted twice-weekly meeting at the Royal Exchange to the present electronic market, spanning the globe on a 24-hour basis. Yet one thing at least has remained unchanged: the principle on which it works. Foreign currencies are switched from one to another at a price which fluctuates second by second; and the place where all this takes place is no different from a market in apples or oranges When pounds are in demand the price goes up: when pounds are sold the price goes down. The only complication worth watching (and one which distinguishes it from other markets) is that the price can be expressed in either currency. The exchange rate, or price, can be shown as so many francs, dollars etc. to one pound, or so many pounds, dollars etc. to 100 francs.

Why Exchange is Needed

Before explaining the way the market works in any detail, however, we need to consider what leads to these demands for different currencies, and how one kind of demand differs from another.

Tourists Each year more foreigners visit Greece, Italy and Spain than Greeks, Italians and Spaniards visit other countries. From June to September their beaches and cities are thronged with foreigners. Where do they obtain the drachmae, lire and pesetas they need? The answer, basically, is that tourists ask their banks and the banks, in turn, obtain some foreign exchange from other tourists and get the rest through the foreign exchange market. Incidentally, we use the phrase 'foreign currency' here to mean either foreign bank notes and cash or foreign bank deposits. The foreign exchange market, basically, concerns itself with bank deposits, between banks, but specialist banks (such as Brown Shipley in London and Swiss Bank Corporation in Zurich) act as wholesale suppliers of notes to other banks.

Importers and Exporters An importer of Japanese cars in California will need to have enough yen at his disposal to pay for the imports, or the Japanese car exporter, if he receives dollars for the cars he has sold, will need to exchange the dollars into yen. Either way there is an extra demand for yen at some point and an additional sale of dollars. As we shall see in a moment, there may be a delay in these transactions because of the use of the forward market. Similar sales and purchases will be going on all round the world. Some of the currency needed may be found within the same bank. In other cases, the bank will have to find what it needs in the market place, that is, in the foreign exchange market.

Investors The demand for currency need not be confined to the sale of services or manufactured goods. Foreign currency will also be needed to purchase a foreign subsidiary or simply a few shares in a foreign company on the New York or Tokyo stock exchange. In recent years the demand for American dollars has been boosted considerably by such purchases. Once again the demands for individual currencies will occasionally be met within an individual bank or security house, but the additional need will have to be satisfied in the foreign exchange market.

Payments by Government The involvement of Governments in making foreign payments has grown dramatically in the past quarter century. At one time only the upkeep of embassies and troop movements led to any significant volume of official payments overseas.

Now governmental involvement covers embassy costs, aid of all kinds, defence costs (including the sale and purchase of armaments on a huge scale) as well as the sale of gold and other national assets. These transactions too lead to demands on the foreign exchange market. To sum up, we have, so far, identified several features of the demands on the foreign exchange market:

(i) Thousands of billions of international payments arise annually because of the need to buy foreign services and foreign goods; to invest abroad; and to make official payments overseas.

(ii) Some of the need for foreign currency, arising from this bewildering array of payments, will be immediately offset by similar payments the other way.

(iii) The banks will meet the demand for individual currencies through their operations in the foreign exchange market, always subject to their own prudence and, in London, the rules of the Bank of England.

(iv) The banks operating in the foreign exchange market are primarily concerned with switching bank deposits in one currency into bank deposits in another currency. They will, however, provide notes and cash, from specialised wholesale banks, where these are needed.

The Market

We finally come to the heart of the matter: the market itself. The difficulty is that, unlike most other city markets, it has no central meeting place but is scattered all round the Square Mile, the participants linked to each other electronically by telephone, telex and information screens.

Who are the participants? At present some 350 banks are permitted to join the market, though the main activity takes place in around 50 of the banks, along with between ten and twelve broking firms (of which seven are specialists in certain currencies).

The individual offices are remarkably equipped. Banks of screens surround each dealer, some containing general economic information, some recording changes in exchange rates and interest rates. Telexes and teleprinters are both prominent. But at the centre of it all is the ubiquitous telephone equipment, specially designed for the purpose, with winking lights and the other marvels of the modern age, linking one bank with another, with the broking firms and the Bank of England in London and with other dealers in other centres overseas. Push buttons summon the contact the dealer wants.

Barclays Bank's foreign exchange dealing room (Harrison Worth Photography)

Each set of dealers in the large banks concentrates on individual currencies, such as the dollar, the mark or the yen. Each bank will have its own buying and selling needs as it begins each day. Some will be on behalf of customers; some on behalf of itself, since it will need to adjust the stock of currencies it maintains for its own purposes. Each dealer will also be responding to calls from others.

As the dealing day begins, around 8 a.m. in London, calls to and from Tokyo, Hong Kong and Singapore will mingle with London and European business. The Middle East centres too will be joining in. Shortly after lunch-time, New York calls will begin to be put through and, later in the afternoon, early business from Los Angeles and San Francisco.

One deal will lead to another. The latest news (of economic trends in the US and Japan; or rises in interest rates in Paris) will bring a further flurry of business. Forward transactions will affect current exchange rates. The incomprehensible jargon; shouts across the room; the winking lights; the need to log each transaction often running into millions—all suggest the need for alertness, stamina and youth. And in fact most dealers these days are in their twenties and thirties.

How the Market Works

We need to distinguish between the brokers and the banks (i.e. the dealers) at the outset. The brokers earn a fee from bringing buyers and sellers together and they do this by providing regular information on the different rates (buying and selling) offered by different banks. Banks can, of course, deal direct with each other.

The rates quoted these days are invariably against one currency, the US dollar. They are called spot rates of exchange and imply that the two currencies concerned will be exchanged on the second working day after the transactions. Two prices are offered by a bank, or a broker on behalf of a bank. For example, a bank will say it will deal in sterling at $1.7995–1.8005. This means it is prepared to buy pounds at a rate of $1.7995 to the pound and to sell pounds at $1.8005 to the pound.

A bank wanting to sell dollars on behalf of a commercial client will receive a range of different possibilities through a broker (or occasionally by direct contact) and will quickly decide which is best. But the amounts on offer may not tally and this imbalance may lead to other deals. And so the market's business will continue.

Forward Market

This, however, is only part of the full story. Exporters and importers will often need to bear in mind that they will be receiving, or paying, foreign currency three, or even six months later, because of delays in deliveries of goods. They will not know, though they may have a view about, the likely exchange rate in three or six months time.

The question facing a British exporter who has agreed a dollar price for his exports at the present rate of exchange between pounds and dollars, is whether he will receive the same amount in pounds when the American importer makes his payment three months hence. If the pound is weaker, he will receive more pounds for the agreed amount of dollars. If it is stronger, he will receive less. How can he avoid this kind of future risk? The answer lies in the use of forward exchange. He can sell American dollars forward at a price. It is in essence the cost of an insurance policy, thus protecting him against any change in the exchange rate.

This is the problem facing the exporter. Now let's see how his decision to sell his dollars forward affects the dealers in the exchange market. In order to meet the exporter's needs to sell his dollars, say, three months forward, the bank dealing in the foreign exchange market can accommodate him in two different ways:

(i) It can borrow dollars for three months, sell them immediately for sterling and put the pounds on deposit for three months. After three months the sterling deposit will be available to pay the exporter, and the bank can repay its dollar loan with the dollars which it arranged to buy from the exporter.

(ii) Alternatively, the bank can buy *spot* sterling and then arrange what is known as a 'swap', exchanging the *spot* sterling for three months' forward sterling. In this case, the two *spot* sterling deals cancel each other out and the bank is left with a contract to receive sterling in three months time. These match the contract with the exporter.

This is all rather complex, even to explain. But it is worth stressing two simple points: that the aim is to provide the exporter with a method of covering his exposure to foreign exchange fluctuations and that the introduction of a 'swap' arrangement by the bank (the second of the two lines of action open to the bank set out above) is based on the use of the short-term money market, which we explained in Chapter 7. It becomes clear, therefore, that it is easier to arrange forward currency deals in currencies where an extensive range of short-term securities and instruments exists. These are basically dollars, pounds and Deutschemarks.

Size of the Market

London's foreign exchange market now has the world's largest turnover, with New York running at about 68 per cent of London's total. The reason for this is partly historical (the widespread use of sterling in the past and the expertise acquired over the years), partly geographical (as we have noted, London is placed neatly in the time zones between the Far East and North America) and partly structural (London has far more foreign banks than other centres). Turnover is colossal. The Bank of England puts it at $187 billion *a day* in London alone. Since world trade in goods and services amounts to only $13.5 billion each working day, turnover in the exchange market between market participants is clearly boosted for other reasons.

The reasons are not far to seek. In the first place, the lending banks making up the market generate exchange business of their own in their capacity as market-makers in different currencies, assuming that they have sufficient stocks for their purpose. On top of this, the world's central banks also operate in the market (often through chosen commercial banks) not only in their role as custodians of national exchange reserves but in attempting to smooth out excessive fluctuations in the market. Finally, as the US dollar is the pivotal currency, transactions between other currencies may involve an intermediate exchange into dollars, again enlarging total turnover. Whatever the reason for this extra turnover, it helps to provide the essential liquidity needed in any active market.

How the EMS Operates

One example of the official influences affecting the foreign exchange market has been the development of the European Monetary System (EMS) and sterling's role in it. Basically the EMS grew out of an attempt to reduce the fluctuations in exchange rates between the currencies of member states of the European Community. The framework was agreed in 1978 and it began to operate in 1979. Although Britain has always participated in the EMS institutional arrangements, sterling did not become a member of the Exchange Rate Mechanism (ERM), which keeps members' rates of exchange within agreed margins of either 2.25 per cent or 6 per cent, until October 1990.

The connection between ERM and the foreign exchange market is that member countries are required to intervene in the market to prevent their currencies breaching certain agreed limits. This intervention is carried out in the foreign exchange market, directly or indirectly, by central banks.

9. Euro-currencies

What the Market is

Thirty years ago the Euro-currency market did not exist. Now it is a fund of credit and capital equivalent to some $5,500 billions. It probably began in Paris, was nurtured and developed in London and now links the leading financial centres of the world.

It is based on a simple and familiar principle: the use of someone else's debts to finance developments world-wide. As we found in Chapter 2, the IOUs of the Irish, once they were regarded as acceptable, in the midst of a bank strike, began to be used as a means of payment by others. So in the international arena, dollars or other currencies, accumulating in the hands of foreigners, began to be lent to others again because they were acceptable. In other words, currency deposits accumulating outside their country of origin, which are basically that country's debts, are being used as the basis of future loans.

The source of such funds will become clearer if we take the case of a French exporter earning dollars from the shipment of goods to the United States. Let's assume that he sells tractors to an American farmer and earns $500,000. He can do several things with the dollars:

- buy American goods or services;
- invest them in American stocks or shares on Wall Street;
- ask his bank to exchange them for French francs;
- exchange them for other foreign currencies, yen, pounds, marks, etc.;
- buy other foreign goods or services;
- hold them in an account outside the USA for future use.

If he chooses one of the first two options, $500,000 will end up back in the United States and thus be extinguished as a foreign-held debt of the US. But if he chooses any of the next three options, the dollars will probably be transferred to another foreign holder or bank who will then face the same original options.

The rapidity with which a major international financial market can be established is graphically shown by the first use in print of the word 'Euro-dollar'.

As this chapter explains, the market in Euro-dollars had developed in the late 1950's. Towards the middle of October 1960, as Financial Editor of *The Times*, I was preparing an annual survey for *The Times*, summing up both the previous year and the prospects, in one of the world major financial centres. 'Challenge of the City's New Freedom: Problems of the Sixties' was the heading.

Turning to the City of London's financial innovations, I began to describe a 'completely new' market which, I explained 'illustrates the true versatility of the City as much as anything that has happened in recent years'. The article went on: 'This is the *so-called Euro-dollar market* ... basically this is a market where dollar deposits earned and owned by foreigners (mostly European as the name implies) can be left and still earn a higher rate of interest than is available in New York'.

I was in effect describing the birth of a market which now dominates the world's financial centres. What I did not realise was that this was the first time the phase 'Euro-dollar market' had been used in public print. It took another twelve years before this 'world first' was finally recognised by the 1972 Supplement to the *Oxford English Dictionary*.

It is when the last option is chosen, i.e. the placing of the dollars in a foreign currency account for future use, either by the original earner of the dollars or by a subsequent recipient of them, that they become available for use by banks in the so-called Euro-currency market. At this point the $500,000 can be lent to others for three, six or twelve months. They have, in current terminology, become active Euro-dollars. If the original exporter had earned yen or marks, and had deposited them, in the same way, outside their country of origin, we would call them Euro-yen or Euro-marks.

How it Began

We now need to explore how, why and when Euro-dollars, Euro-yen, Euro-marks emerged in the first place and why the 'Euro-' tag has always been attached to them.

We have to go back to the Europe of the mid-1950s to find the answer. Marshal Aid dollars were flowing to Europe. Its major economies were beginning to emerge successfully from the destruction of war. The stirrings of the future Common Market were already discernible. Trading and currency barriers were being slowly dismantled.

As a result, Europe's foreign earnings were rising again and the dollar deficit it had been plagued with for close on a decade was moving into surplus. US dollars were thus accumulating in European hands, at a time when the freedom to switch currencies across national frontiers was returning.

Our earlier example of the choice facing the French exporter, earning surplus dollars, was becoming commonplace. Enterprising financial institutions began to recognise new credit opportunities, and to find ways of using the spare dollars. Where the first on lending of such surplus dollar deposits began is still disputed, but it is now generally accepted that the Soviet-owned bank in Paris, Banque Commerciale pour l'Europe du Nord, is a leading contender for the title. Its telex 'answer-back' code was 'Euro-bank' and, when it was offering dollars, the term 'Euro-dollar' was an easy adaptation.

Yet the Euro-dollar market we know was not developed in Paris. The vast international credit potential lying behind the dollars accumulating in European hands was first recognised in London, not Paris, primarily among the British overseas and merchant banks and the branches of American banks. They quickly began to bid (that is, offer higher interest rates) for the surplus dollars and were helped by an official quirk in New York. Under a financial regulation ('Q'), introduced to curb excessive interest rates for house loans, banks in New York were prevented from offering interest rates above a certain level.

So what New York prevented, London encouraged, and by the end of the 1950s a new source of international finance had been tapped and was being slowly developed in London. But it was not immediately recognised and it was not until 1960 that the first public reference to the phrase 'Euro-dollar' was made. The first recorded reference, according to the 1972 Supplement to the *Oxford English Dictionary*, was in *The Times'* financial review of 24 October 1960.

How it Works

A new source of international money had been discovered, just when the world economic boom of the sixties and early seventies was beginning. Soon foreign banks were flocking to London to take advantage of these new facilities. The nucleus of the Euro-currency market was quickly formed and the present-day techniques emerged from the simple three-month and six-month dollar credits of those early days.

In the early 1960s, the Euro-currency market divided itself into two different sectors: (i) that providing *Euro-currency loans*; and (ii) that providing *Euro-bonds*. The first was in essence a credit market supplied directly by banks; the second was an international capital market offered by banks as an alternative to the national capital markets.

The distinction between international credit supplied by banks and an international capital market based on the issue of market instruments (Euro-bonds etc.) is worth noting, for, as we shall see in a moment, the dividing line between the two has lately begun to get more and more blurred.

(i) Euro-currency Loans   In the case of loans, the necessary currency funds were originally sought from holders on a three-month or six-month basis. Through the use of what are called 'roll-over' techniques (which amount to little more than the renewal of existing deposits), funds were held for longer periods, thus enabling the banks acting as intermediaries to lengthen the Euro-currency loans to borrowers. In the early years such loans were extended up to two years; but, with the introduction of new techniques (especially the use of variable interest rates), the length of loans moved to five years, then seven years and beyond.

The interest rate offered to holders of external currency deposits is based on what is known as LIBOR, that is the London Interbank Offered Rate. This rate naturally varies. When these funds are lent to borrowers in the Euro-currency market, a margin is added to the LIBOR rate to cover administrative costs and the potential risks.

Borrowers pay a flexible rate of interest and can take up as much, or as little, of the loan as they wish.

(ii) Euro-bonds   Just as the American Regulation Q gave an unexpected boost to the development of the Euro-dollar market outside the United States, so the imposition of an interest equalisation tax on foreign bond issues in New York in 1963 (which raised the cost of borrowing money there to foreign borrowers) was a powerful boost to Euro-bonds.

Instead of issuing dollar bonds in New York, international banks, spurred on by their successes with the Euro-currency loans, turned to issuing dollar bonds in several centres simultaneously. They were the first Euro-bonds. American banks in particular were encouraged to issue such bonds abroad which, for close on a decade, they were unable to do at home.

Euro-bonds were originally mainly in dollars. Thus foreign corporations were able to raise fixed-interest-rate dollar loans, in the form of bonds, in, say, London and Luxembourg simultaneously. They would be for a fixed period, from five to fifteen years. And the international banks naturally tapped some of the same Euro-currency market sources for their potential purchasers: foreign corporations and governments and rich individuals.

Where the Market Operates

Thus, within a decade culminating in the mid-1960s, two new additions were added to the world's financial instruments: Eurocurrency loans and Euro-bonds. Both have taken their place alongside the nationally based credits and bonds.

In each case, international banks operating out of leading financial centres such as London, New York, Frankfurt, Zurich, Paris and Tokyo and out of more recently established centres such as Hong Kong, Singapore, Nassau, Bahrain and Luxembourg, have co-operated together in syndicates.

Euro-credits have usually involved one international bank as lead manager, with one or two others as co-managers and often a score or more other banks as participants. Similarly with Euro-bonds, one bank will be lead manager and scores of others will act as underwriters of the issue.

But where, you may ask, is the Euro-currency market itself? Where exactly does it operate? There is in fact no market-place, like the Stock Exchange. It is held together by telephone, telex and fax, and operates, simultaneously, from several centres.

In London, where it was developed and where its major developments are still initiated, day-to-day activities, particularly the deposit-raising, take place in the foreign exchange operations rooms of the major banks. But the construction of Euro-syndicated loans and Euro-bonds goes on in a variety of bank parlours, and security houses, linked together by world-wide telex and fax.

The *secondary* market in Euro-bonds or the more recent Floating Rate Notes (that is, where existing bonds or notes are traded) takes place between banks and security houses, largely in London, New York and Luxembourg. All Euro-bond issues are quoted on a European Stock Exchange.

The Borrowers

So far we have been primarily concerned with the world banks supplying and building up these new international markets. They were naturally crucial in the initial development of the markets. More recently, however, the needs of the borrowers have begun to play a more significant influence in market developments.

The original borrowers were the credit-worthy multinationals, large industrial companies and governments of the industrialised west. Individual central banks too used the Euro-currency market as a safety valve, sometimes lending surplus dollars, sometimes borrowing. All this was in the economic boom period of the sixties and early seventies.

Following the dramatic rise in oil prices in 1973–74, however, new financial problems arose. Huge currency surpluses began to accumulate in the Middle East, and western banks were urged to 're-cycle' (i.e. to borrow and re-lend) them to the needy countries of the developing world, through the technique of syndicated loans. Otherwise, it was said, economic and social disaster would spread throughout South America and South East Asia.

International banks initially dithered, wondering (rightly as it turned out) whether it would be wise to borrow such surpluses and re-lend them to the developing world and thus take on the political risk, rather than persuade the Middle East holders to lend direct. But the combination of competition (if Bank A would not do it, Bank B certainly would) and the persuasive powers of politicians and commentators alike, calmed all doubts and in a space of six years, Euro-credits of all kinds flowed to the developing world and the Soviet bloc. At a later stage, the need to spread the risk on loan portfolios was a further stimulus to lending.

We now know the results. International banks clearly lent too much to the wrong countries at the wrong time. By the autumn of 1982, some of the largest borrowers—Poland, Mexico, Brazil, Argentina—were having difficulties in making the regular interest payments, let alone repaying loans when due.

The debts built up so rapidly in the late 1970s and early 1980s through Euro-currency lending have thus left their mark on lenders and borrowers alike. Although the capital basis of leading international banks has been undermined as provisions have had to be put aside to meet potential losses, Japan's payment surpluses have in some ways replaced the oil country surpluses, and continuing US deficits have left surplus dollars available for international lending. At the same time past borrowers have been keen to lengthen repayment periods and to re-arrange their future liabilities. Industrial borrowers have tended to replace Sovereign country borrowers.

New Techniques

Thus the climate has been ripe for the introduction of new lending techniques and more flexible financial instruments. The Euro-markets have responded with a bewildering array of new processes, with equally bewildering names, from 'swaps' to FRNs and ECPs and from RUFs, PUFs and NIFs to SNIFs, MOFs and PIFs. The big banks now spend much time in trying to tailor new techniques to the needs of their international customers.

Text books and individual conferences are now devoted to many of these techniques. All we will try to explain briefly, therefore, is what some of the main techniques attempt to do for the lender or the borrower.

(i) Swaps There are interest rate swaps and currency swaps. Both help a borrower to change the character of his existing debts. This can be achieved either by avoiding an unnecessary concentration of, say, dollar debts or by changing the proportions of debts with fixed or floating interest rates.

A currency swap is usually arranged through a bank, acting as intermediary. One borrower may have excessive dollar debts; another may have excessive Swiss franc debts. The bank can help each borrower to switch a proportion of its debts into the other currency, partly through the use of matching formal exchange contracts, and partly through each borrower's ability to forward the appropriate currency for each other. Each borrower is in effect borrowing the currency in which its credit is best and offering the terms to the other.

An interest rate swap can be done directly between a borrower and a bank. A bank finds it is easier, and cheaper, to borrow fixed-rate credit. An industrial corporation, however, will get better terms from floating-rate credit. So in such a swap, each borrows for the other. In other words, each party is borrowing in the market (floating rate or fixed rate) in which its credit is best and offering the terms to the other (i.e. swapping credit positions).

To understand how each swap is *actually* carried out needs patience, numerous diagrams and an expert (and friendly) banker.

(ii) Floating Rate Notes (FRNs)   As we noted earlier, Euro-credits based on short-term deposits were transformed into larger credits by the simple process of rolling them over, i.e. renewing them at regular intervals at flexible rates of interest. The floating rate note is the result of introducing similar interest rate flexibilities into the bond market. A company borrowing money on such an issue is thus not tied to a fixed rate of interest; nor indeed is the lender.

Although FRNs were first introduced in 1970, only in the last few years have they been used in large volume. Banks themselves have recently been among the main borrowers.

The maturity of FRNs extend from five to fifteen years, and even longer. Interest rates are based on an agreed margin (dependent on the borrower's credit rating) over LIBOR (see earlier), and are adjusted at regular intervals. Euro-Commercial Paper (ECP) has also established itself as an alternative method of finance.

(iii) RUFs, NIFs, MOFs, etc.   These various facilities have different descriptions, e.g. revolving underwriting facilities (RUFs), note issuing facilities (NIFs), Multi-Option Facilities (MOFs), etc., etc., but their aim, and the principles behind them, are much the same. Borrowers are receiving a basic, medium-term flexible facility. This in turn is financed by the purchase by investors of short-term notes, usually of three or six months' duration. The banks ensure that the short-term notes link together to provide a medium-term facility. They do this by underwriting the underlying short-term notes (i.e. by promising to buy any unpurchased notes) and by providing a stand-by credit. The term 'Note issuance facility', or NIF, is often used to cover all the different variants, such as Euro-note facilities, or revolving underwriting facilities (RUFs).

(iv) Euro-Equities   Although the Euro-currency and Euro-bond markets were originally built on the provision of credit and fixed interest capital, it was clearly only a matter of time before domestic equities (that is, the issue of ordinary shares) would be followed by international issues, now called Euro-equities. They have expanded rapidly in recent years and now offer large international corporations an additional source of equity finance.

(v) Mezzanine Debt   This has basically been associated with corporate restructuring in Europe and North America. In cases where companies are acquired with borrowed funds, the borrowing can include some form of subordinated debt. In Europe this involves bank debt with equity warrants attached, and in the US, high-yielding bonds.

We noted that the Euro-currency market split into two sections in the early 1960s, one supplying credits (Euro-syndicated loans) through banks direct to borrowers, the other providing capital market instruments (Euro-bonds). That distinction has begun to be blurred by recent developments and by the introduction of some of the new techniques we have just described. Thus the basis of a medium-term Euro-credit can now be a note, which is marketable and transferable, rather than a deposit. Thus banks are more able to adjust their lending to suit their existing liabilities. The challenge of the international debt crisis has produced new instruments and new flexibilities.

10. The Gold Market

Markets in gold bring together rich governments and thrifty peasants; dentists and investors; capitalist banks and Communist trading organisations. They are markets in a commodity and markets in money. Most leading financial centres have one.

What Gold is

Gold is a unique commodity. It remains the basic store of value in the world—for governments and individuals. It is widely regarded as the main bulwark against rampant inflation, depreciating currencies, revolution and invasion. It has a glamour possessed by no other metal. Yet its price, whether in terms of other commodities or paper money, can be as volatile as anything else.

It is a metal with remarkable qualities: soft enough to be turned into beautiful jewellery; hard enough to be used as the basis of coins. Its possession has fostered political strength over the centuries, from Alexander to Hitler and from Croesus to Haile Selassie. Its history reflects human psychology.

Markets in Gold

London has had a gold market of sorts for centuries—ever since the merchanting classes began to show their growing commercial strength. The goldsmiths began as processors of gold, gradually becoming holders of gold and, eventually, as we saw in Chapter 2, embryo bankers.

Throughout these developments, they naturally dealt in gold and made a market in gold. But it was hardly the gold market we know today; and between then and now came the century and more of the gold standard and the subsequent gold exchange standard when, for quite different reasons, the London gold market price was also not as free as it has since become.

Uses of Gold

Behind these developments lie the uses to which mankind has put gold: as a form of money; as an adornment; and as an industrial ingredient.

Since gold was first mined about 4000 BC, it is estimated that some 100,000 tons have been dug out of the ground—mainly in South Africa, California, Alaska, Russia, Canada and Australia. Of this tonnage, about a third is now in official hands as national gold reserves. The rest is in private hands (basically around necks and arms, in mouths, under beds or in banks), in industrial use or simply lost.

Thus the use of gold for private purposes has competed with its use for official monetary purposes. While the first has encouraged an opening up of freer gold markets, the latter has often led to restrictions on the movement of market prices.

From 1815 (the end of the Napoleonic wars) to 1914, the western world was basically on a gold standard or at least Britain, the leading industrial nation, was. This implied that Britain was obliged to pay gold in exchange for its international debts at fixed prices, and that a link existed between its gold reserves and the volume of its internal currency. Other countries such as France, Germany and the United

Gold		
Who Sells: Who Buys		
(1990 in tons)		
Supply of Gold		*Demand for Gold*
South Africa	605	Jewellery	1,986
United States	295	Electronics	143
Australia	241	Other fabrication	252
Canada	165		
Brazil	78	Official sector purchases	40
Philippines	37	Bar hoarding	236
Rest of non-Communist world	313	'Investment'	144
Communist bloc	380		
Old gold scrap	441		
Gold loans	5		
Forward sales	240		
TOTAL	2,799	TOTAL	2,799

Source: *Gold 1991*, published by Gold Fields Mineral Services Ltd

States adopted the gold standard discipline for certain spells. Since 1919 individual nations have moved from the gold standard to a so-called gold exchange standard (under which individual currencies were linked to gold) and, since 1973, to a system only loosely based on gold.

The London gold market has reflected these changes directly. When Britain was on the gold standard, the London gold market price could only move between the statutory buying and selling prices of the Bank of England. The movement in effect reflected changes between sterling and other foreign currencies. The gold market was thus in reality a part of the foreign exchange market, or rather the international market in commercial bills.

Once the gold standard was finally abandoned in 1931, no such official buying and selling prices for gold existed until the United States adopted a gold exchange standard in 1934, under which the US was obliged to buy gold offered to it at $35 an ounce. With this modified arrangement in place, the London gold price was also once more restricted in its potential movement.

In effect, the gold price could hardly drop below $35 an ounce or its sterling equivalent. If it did so, for any length of time, it would pay people to buy gold in London and offer it to the US Treasury at the official price of $35. In addition, the fixed rate of exchange between the US dollar and the pound, which prevailed until 1971, ensured further stability in the sterling price of gold.

London Market

The London gold market as we now know it was opened in 1919 and closed between 1939 and 1954. When it re-opened in the spring of 1954, it quickly re-established itself as the largest in the world.

The reason was simple. The world's largest gold producer, South Africa, arranged to sell the bulk of her output through London, as did Canada, Australia and the United States. In addition, the Soviet Union, the world's second largest producer, used London dealers to sell a large part of her sales. Moreover, the world's central banks also made most of their official gold dealings through the London market. These dealings were originally a matter of re-adjusting the size of national holdings, reflecting the ebb and flow of international trade. But from 1960 onwards, the world's leading central banks deliberately bought and sold gold on the London market as an official pool in attempts to curb speculative movements in the gold price. The Bank of England ran this official consortium.

In fact these attempts to control the gold price eventually failed and in the first half of March 1968, after selling no less than $3,000 million worth of gold in a fortnight in attempts to offset an unprecedented speculative demand for gold, the official Gold Pool gave up the attempt. The Governor of the Bank of England closed the London gold market on 15 March and flew to Washington to meet other central bank governors to consider what to do next. They eventually decided to stop their official interventions in the market, and to create a two-tier system which would accommodate (i) official dealings among central banks and (ii) free-market dealings. The first maintained the official US price of gold; the second was allowed to reflect private demand.

This was yet a further example of the way in which official uses of gold interfered with, and restricted, what was in effect a private gold market. Thus the London market, which had attracted the bulk of official gold dealings, suffered accordingly. It was closed for a fortnight—from 15 March to 1 April 1968. And, not surprisingly, found that the Zurich gold market had stolen a good slice of the world's business in its absence. Middle East and Far Eastern demand had switched to Switzerland and so too had South African supplies, for a variety of reasons, some political, some financial. What was to be a decade and a half of intense rivalry between London and Zurich had begun.

One final move freeing the London market price from undue official restraints was needed; and it came in 1971 when the United States effectively devalued the US dollar and, at the same time, severed its direct link with gold.

How the Market Works

Throughout these remarkable international gyrations, the modern London gold market had continued to operate in much the same way as it did, originally, on 12 September 1919. Rothschild's still house the market and still provide the market's daily chairman. Even the main participants are almost the same: N. M. Rothschild (founded 1804); Mocatta and Goldsmid (1684); Sharps, Pixley (Sharps founded in 1750 and merged with Pixley in 1852); and Samuel Montagu (1853), with Mase Westpac having taken the place of Johnson Matthey.

In 1987 this inner core of members decided to form the London Bullion Market Association and the new structure and membership were agreed in April 1988. Members now total 61. Eleven are accepted as 'market-makers'. The remaining 50 are classified as 'ordinary members'. Market-makers are supervised by the Bank of England. Members are drawn from the major gold centres world-wide—including Zurich, Frankfurt, Sydney, Tokyo and New York. The Bank of China is a member.

Gold price fixing at the offices of N. M. Rothschild & Co. (Colour Chrome Studios)

The five main members meet twice a day (at 10.30 a.m. and 3.00 p.m.) in the portrait-lined room at Rothschild's in New Court, a small courtyard in a narrow City street, close to the Bank of England. The portraits of several European monarchs are a daily reminder of Rothschild's early financial history.

This then is where the world's demand for, and supply of, gold comes to a head daily and produces a morning and an afternoon 'fixing', the latter specifically geared to North American dealings later in the day. The market in fact continues from 8 a.m. to 5 p.m., both before and after the 'fixing'.

The daily fixing is the price at which the five market members are able to agree they will satisfy the outstanding buying and selling orders for gold. To achieve such an agreed price, the members sit at individual desks round the room. Each member has his own buying and selling orders before him and is in telephonic communication with his office throughout the session. Before and after the fixing all members deal with each other without paying value added tax, provided that the physical delivery of gold is not effected outside the membership.

The chairman from Rothschild's conducts each session and attempts to find a price at which outstanding buying and selling orders can be matched. Each member has a small Union Jack on his desk. So long as the flag remains upright, the dealer is unwilling to agree to the suggested price. When all flags have been lowered, indicating assent, the price is 'fixed' and immediately published world-wide.

There are several advantages in channeling orders through the 'fixing' process. The spread between buying and selling prices is narrow. The seller is assured of the 'fixing' price and the buyer pays a small commission in addition to the 'fixing' price. The agreed price at each fixing is based on actual transactions and can be used as such in legal negotiations. The world's central banks use it to value their gold reserves.

Competition

It is difficult to assess whether London or Zurich now undertakes the biggest turnover in gold. Apart from the capabilities of the individual dealing firms, several factors still favour London's operations:

- London now has the greatest concentration of wholesale market-makers in gold in the world.
- The market is supervised directly by the Bank of England.
- The London market's so-called Good Delivery list of melters and assayers whose marks are acceptable world-wide, thus ensuring quality control.
- The role of the Bank of England in storing bullion for other central banks, a role only rivalled by the Federal Reserve Bank of New York.
- London's time zone advantage, coupled with London dealers' subsidiaries in Hong Kong, Sydney, Singapore and New York, the other main trading centres outside Europe.
- The acceptance of London's spot quotation, known as gold 'loco-London'. This is 'for delivery London', enhances the role of London in handling physical gold and ensures that it acts as the clearing centre for the international market.
- London is the only market to publish a Gold LIBOR for one, two, six and twelve months. (See Chapter 9 for an explanation of LIBOR.)

The generation of business, especially from the Middle Eastern and Far Eastern markets, plainly depends on the maintenance of secrecy. Security too is a prime factor. So detailed figures of imports and exports of gold bullion are not published. But London dealers now estimate that the London market turns over between $1 billion and $2 billion worth of gold weekly and that London takes 40 per cent of the world gold business and Zurich 30 per cent.

11. Commodity Markets

What They Are

A maritime nation, trading manufactured goods for commodities, attracts markets where such raw materials can be bought and sold. London's markets thus developed as a natural adjunct to trade. They have continued as natural indicators of world prices. And they have spawned a variety of futures markets, which we shall describe in the next chapter.

The commodity markets we are concerned with vary considerably in the way they operate, mainly reflecting the commodities themselves. Some, like furs, tea or feathers, are of varying quality. Others, like copper or tin, can be of standardised quality. Thus some need auction techniques; others simply an open outcry forum.

The main markets can be divided into the following categories:

Exchanges: (for sale of sugar, cocoa, copper, coffee, etc.)— Competitive outcry system with standardised qualities.
Sale Rooms: (for the sale of spices, nuts, fibres, etc.)—Deals between agents, representing buyers and sellers.
Auctions: (for the sale of tea, furs, etc.)—Competitive bidding, after examination.

How They Work

It is the exchanges, that is the world markets for 'hard' and 'soft' commodities, that we shall be primarily concerned with in this chapter. The 'hard' commodities include the non-ferrous metals such as lead, zinc and copper, and the 'soft' commodities coffee, cocoa and sugar. The hard commodities are administered by the London Metal Exchange and the soft commodities by the London Futures and Options Exchange (London FOX).

The main 'hard' and 'soft' commodities are traded in what are known as 'rings'. The dealers sit in an arranged circle and during the

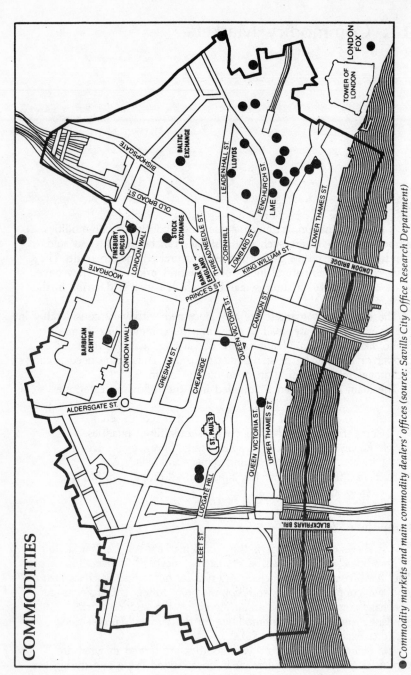

COMMODITIES

BISHOPSGATE

OLD BROAD ST

BALTIC EXCHANGE

LEADENHALL ST

LLOYDS

FENCHURCH ST

LME

TOWER OF LONDON

LONDON FOX

LOWER THAMES ST

LONDON BRIDGE

STOCK EXCHANGE

THREADNEEDLE ST

FINSBURY CIRCUS

LONDON WALL

BANK OF ENGLAND

PRINCE S ST

CORNHILL

LOMBARD ST

KING WILLIAM ST

MOORGATE

QUEEN VICTORIA ST

CANNON ST

BARBICAN CENTRE

LONDON WALL

GRESHAM ST

CHEAPSIDE

ALDERSGATE ST

ST. PAUL'S

QUEEN VICTORIA ST

UPPER THAMES ST

LUDGATE HILL

BLACKFRIARS BRI.

FLEET ST

• Commodity markets and main commodity dealers' offices (source: Savills City Office Research Department)

individual sessions bid verbally between each other. Hence the description an open 'outcry system'. Those seated around the ring, who are enabled to deal, are representatives of ring-dealing firms. Many are based overseas.

At the London Metal Exchange, clerks man the telephones immediately behind the ring, passing on the latest market information, receiving new market orders and transmitting the latest deals and prices. In addition inter-office trading also takes place with the use of electronic equipment. The offices in turn will be in telephone or telex communication with business contacts world-wide.

These official sessions undertake three basic operations:

- They enable commodities to be bought and sold, under guaranteed conditions.
- They enable world price quotations to be established in an open market place.
- They offer hedging facilities—means of protection against sharp changes in prices, which we shall be exploring more closely in the next chapter.

A distinction has to be made between the metals and the soft commodities. Whereas deals in copper, zinc, lead, aluminium, nickel and silver are traded on a daily basis up to three months ahead, others offer longer-term futures. Secondly, while there is an obligation on members to acquire or deliver physical *metal* on the specified date of a contract, no similar obligation attaches to other commodities.

These distinctions basically reflect the rules and regulations of the different associations governing commodity dealings in the Square Mile. It is necessary, therefore, to outline separately the individual roles played by the various bodies involved.

London Metal Exchange   The Exchange has its own Board of Directors and operates its daily metal markets in Plantation House, Fenchurch Street. These operate between 11.45 a.m. and 1.25 p.m. and, in the afternoon, between 3.20 p.m. and 5 p.m.

Each of the six metals (copper, zinc, lead, aluminium, nickel and tin) is allotted two trading sessions of five minutes each, in the morning and afternoon. What are known as 'kerb' dealings in all the metals take place for twenty minutes after the morning and afternoon sessions.

The 'official' prices for prompt and forward delivery are monitored by a quotations committee and announced after the morning session. These prices are used by producer countries and the majority of the world's industry for pricing raw materials.

There are 21 ring dealing members at present. Of these, over 80 per cent are owned or partly owned by overseas companies. They have an obligation to receive or deliver physical metal, according to contract, unless the transaction has been 'squared' by a corresponding contract the other way. The physical deliveries are made by the presentation of warrants at L.M.E. registered warehouses in the UK, Continental Europe, Singapore and the USA.

London Futures and Options Exchange (London FOX)   This is the centre for 'soft' commodities—cocoa, robusta coffee, raw and white sugar. London FOX is responsible for the futures and traded options markets in these commodities as well as administration, management and communications. It also provides market premises and services for the International Petroleum Exchange and the Cocoa Association of London. There are currently fifty 'local' memberships available for private individuals.

International Petroleum Exchange   As a response to the increased volatility of energy prices, the International Petroleum Exchange of London was incorporated in November 1980. It is Europe's first and largest energy futures exchange. It provides futures contracts in Brent crude oil, Dubai sour crude oil, gas oil, Naphtha and heavy fuel oil. Traded options are also available in Brent crude oil and gas oil. The exchange is situated at Commodity Quay in St. Katherine's Dock.

London Clearing House   This is essentially a service organisation enabling the various markets to operate successfully. The LCH provides a totally independent guarantee, being owned by six leading British banks (Barclays, Lloyds, Midland, National Westminster, Standard Chartered and Royal Bank of Scotland).

The primary role of the LCH is to guarantee contract performance by becoming the central counterparty to all contracts registered in the names of its clearing members. This enables clearing members to settle their obligations without any reference to the other original contracting parties and thus provide a basic assurance to clearing members that individual obligations will be fulfilled.

LCH clears both options and futures contracts for the London Futures and Options Exchange (London FOX), the International Petroleum Exchange (IPE), the London International Financial Futures Exchange (LIFFE) and the London Metal Exchange (LME).

It also provides management services to enable the clearing of the London Traded Options Market (LTOM) through the London Options Clearing House (LOCH).

LCH is dedicated to the promotion and growth of the London derivatives markets in the international arena.

Basic Facilities   It is time to remind ourselves what these different organisations are providing for customers. Both producers and consumers of commodities are given certain basic facilities in the London markets:

● Markets for arranging sales and purchases of individual commodities.
● World spot and futures prices on a daily basis.
● Clearing arrangements and trading guarantees.
● Futures and option facilities.

How the futures markets work now needs to be considered separately, in a chapter of its own.

12. Forwards, Futures, Options, ...

Prices in free markets can go up and down. This is just as true of currencies, securities, bonds and other financial instruments, as it is of second-hand cars, apples or copper. In the past decade and a half, both exchange rates and interest rates have been more volatile than at any time since the Second World War. Commodity prices too have hardly been stable.

Not surprisingly, the City's markets, like their counterparts in Chicago and New York, have begun to provide (or in some cases, improve) ways of reducing the risks which accompany such gyrations. They have done this by the development of facilities such as forward markets, futures markets and option markets.

In some cases, these markets have simply revived old pre-war habits such as in the forward exchange markets and the security option markets. In others, new facilities have been introduced, especially in the futures markets in financial instruments such as Government securities, Euro-currencies and the like.

What They Do

Basically these markets offer ways of modifying future or existing risks. They also provide opportunities for outright speculation. The choice is up to the customer, but both functions are needed to give the depth of turnover such markets need.

The first step in understanding what they offer is to differentiate between forward markets, futures markets and option markets.

Forward Markets

These basically operate in the foreign exchange and commodity markets. They offer contracts between one trader and another, promising to buy or sell a specified volume of a commodity or a currency on a certain date. They enable a trader who has an obligation to give or receive an agreed amount (of a commodity or currency) on a future date to protect himself against a fluctuation in the price of that commodity or currency in the interim.

The essential characteristics of a forward contract are: (i) it is undertaken for any required volume, (ii) the commodity or currency is expected to be delivered, (iii) the contract cannot be transferred or sold to second or third parties (i.e. it cannot be 'traded'), (iv) the contract need not be published.

Futures Markets   Like forward markets, they offer a place where contracts are arranged between traders, promising to deliver an agreed amount of a commodity, security or currency on an agreed date, at a price. They offer the same protection as a forward contract.

The essential characteristics of a futures market, in contrast to a forward market are: (i) the contracts are standardised, (ii) business is open and prices published, (iii) the contracts can thus be traded (i.e. the obligations can be subsequently bought and sold), (iv) dealings are usually organised by a clearing house, providing protection to the participants.

The main contracts in the futures markets concern securities, currencies and commodities.

Option Markets   These too concern contracts for future settlement, but the emphasis is on a *right*, which the holder of the option may exercise if he wishes, to buy or sell a commodity, security or currency, not an *obligation* as in the case of forward or futures markets.

They have a terminology of their own. A 'call' option is a right to *buy* and a 'put' option is a right to *sell*. The future price at which the option can be taken is called the 'strike price'.

Option markets are not new. But *traded* option markets on which the rights to buy or sell can be passed on to others are a more recent development.

The main contracts in the option markets concern securities and currencies.

Where They Are

The origin of today's futures markets was probably in Antwerp (in the sixteenth century), followed by Amsterdam (in the seventeenth century) and Chicago (in the nineteenth). Options were developed in London in the nineteenth century. More recent developments have emerged, again, from Chicago and, subsequently, from New York, London, Amsterdam, Sydney, Philadelphia, Paris, Hong Kong, Singapore, Tokyo and Bermuda.

The various markets do not operate from one spot in London, but are scattered over different sections of the Square Mile. Let me therefore, sum up who does what, where:

- *London International Financial Futures Exchange* (LIFFE) offers futures contracts based on UK, US and European short-term interest rates, UK, US, German and Japanese Government bonds, the FT/SE 100 stock index and ECU bonds, and also offers options on financial futures.
- *The London Stock Exchange* offers equity and index options.
- *London Futures and Options Exchange* (London FOX) offers commodity futures and traded options contracts in cocoa, coffee and sugar.
- *London Metal Exchange* (LME) offers commodity hedging contracts.
- *Baltic Exchange* offers shipping freight futures contracts.
- *International Petroleum Exchange* (IPE) offers gas oil, Brent crude oil, Dubai sour crude, Naphtha and heavy fuel oil futures contracts.
- *London Foreign Exchange Market* offers forward currency contracts.
- *International banks* in London offer customised currency option contracts.
- *London Clearing House* (LCH) provides clearing and guarantee facilities for the London derivative markets.

How They Work

Since forward, futures and option markets are available in several different spots and cover several different instruments, it is easier to explain how they work by choosing a typical example in each market.

1. Forward Contracts in Foreign Exchange   Foreign exchange risks have been rising rapidly over the past decade and a half as the fixed exchange rate regime set up at Bretton Woods in 1946 gradually broke down under the combined assault of inflation, oil price decisions, fluctuating interest rates and currency doubts.

This has led to a bigger turnover in the *forward exchange markets* as big corporations, increasingly conscious of their exposure to exchange rate risks, arising from their foreign operations, have felt the need for additional protection.

The risks are of different kinds:

(i) An exporter sells large quantities of his goods to a French buyer at today's prices, but will not be paid in French francs until delivery in three months time. By then the exchange rate may have moved decisively upwards or downwards.

(ii) An importer contracts to buy, say, 5,000 Japanese cars over
the next six months and agrees to pay in six months time at
current Japanese prices. If the pound declines in value over the
following six months, he will have to pay more in pounds to
meet the Japanese cost of the cars.

In each case, one way to offset, or at least limit, the risk arising
from a change in the exchange rate is to buy or sell (depending on
the kind of risk he is running) an equivalent amount of foreign
currency three or six months ahead. The purchase or sales of the
foreign exchange is meant to match the outstanding obligation and is
undertaken for forward delivery at an agreed future date at today's
exchange rate, with a so-called forward premium. The forward
premium is the price paid for protection. It is based on a number of
factors, primarily the difference in interest rates between the two
countries concerned, but also a variety of political and economic
factors likely to affect the demand for and supply of the two
currencies.

The interest rate differential is not difficult to understand. A bank
with £1,000 in London wishing to exchange it into dollars in three
months time, is faced with a choice: it can leave it in London, earning
the London rate of interest of, say, 11 per cent, and then switch it
into dollars in three months time or switch it into dollars now (at the
current rate of exchange) and earn, say, 8 per cent in New York. The
forward exchange rate available will reflect this difference in interest
rates as well as other factors.

2. Option Contracts in Securities Options are remarkably flexible
in their application. When used in conjunction with securities, they can
help to protect an existing holding of shares against a marked drop in
share prices; to protect an investor in a variety of other ways; or
simply to encourage a speculative venture.

It is useful to repeat exactly what the different options imply. 'Call'
options give the right to buy shares at a previously agreed price (to
help the memory think of them as 'calling' the shares from their
original owner). 'Put' options provide a facility to sell shares at an
agreed price ('putting' them on to a new owner).

Let us take an example of each.

A shareholder owning 1,000 shares in ICI may fear that the share
price is likely to fall, but may not wish to sell his shares. The option
market will allow him to buy a 'put' option, that is the right to sell his
shares at an agreed price (the prices available are in specified steps). If
the price goes down as he expects, he can *either* take up the option

Future and Option Contracts Available in London (1991)
A. Options

1. *London Stock Exchange*
71 individual securities ⟶ FT/Stock Exchange Index

2. *LIFFE*
Long gilt interest rate futures ⟶ German government bond
US Treasury bond ⟶ Three month Eurodollar
Three month sterling ⟶ Three month Euromark

3. *London FOX*
Cocoa ⟶ Raw sugar
Coffee (Arabica and Robusta) ⟶ White sugar
Soyabean meal

4. *International Petroleum Exchange*
Brent crude oil ⟶ Gas oil

B. Futures

1. *LIFFE*
Long gilt
German government bond
Three month ECU
US Treasury bond
ECU bond
Japanese government bond
FT/SE 100 Stock Index
Three month Eurodollar ⟶ FT/SE Eurotrack 100 Index
Three month sterling ⟶ Three month Euromark
Three month Euro-Swiss franc

2. *London FOX*
Cocoa ⟶ Raw sugar
White sugar ⟶ Coffee (Arabica and Robusta)
Rice ⟶ Grain
Meat ⟶ Soyabean meal
Potatoes

3. *International Petroleum Exchange*
Gas oil ⟶ Heavy fuel oil
Brent crude oil ⟶ Naphtha
Dubai sour crude oil

4. *London Metal Exchange*
Copper ⟶ Nickel
Lead ⟶ Aluminium
Zinc ⟶ Silver

to sell the shares at the chosen price (i.e. at a higher price than in the depressed market) or he can sell the 'put' option, again at a profit. The reason for the profit on the 'put' option is that 'put' options rise in value as prices decline, whereas 'call' options do the opposite (i.e. they rise when share prices rise). If the shares had risen, his shares would be worth more and he would simply allow the 'put' option to lapse, having paid a small premium for protection against a fall.

Take another example, the case of an investor who expects a share price to go up before he has the resources to buy in the market. In these circumstances, he can buy a 'call' option, which will allow him the right to buy his shares at an agreed price in the future. If the price rises, so does the value of his options. He then has a choice depending on circumstances. He can take up his option and buy the shares at the favourable price (i.e. lower than the increased one in the market) *or* he can sell the options at their higher value.

One point worth grasping about options is the effect of 'gearing', a term we have already met in the case of investment trusts. Since an option costs only a fraction of the price of a share and since option prices tend to move in line with share prices, the *percentage* changes in option prices are inevitably greater than in the underlying share prices. It means that big profits *and big losses* can quickly be realised, unless the investor is clear what he is doing.

The conclusion to be drawn is simple: before plunging into the option market, get a wet towel, a good adviser and ask yourself these questions (as the Stock Exchange itself advises) at the outset:

● What is my purpose: protection or speculation?
● How much capital can I afford to risk?
● How long should I wait before deciding to act during the period of an option?

3. Futures Contracts in Commodities and Securities These contracts began in commodities and have been extended to securities, currencies and shipping freights. In each case the aims of operators are the same: to protect an existing situation against any adverse future change in prices or to speculate.

The positions that need protection vary considerably:

● A manufacturer who has ordered raw materials in advance at agreed prices fears a drop in prices.
● A manufacturer who has agreed to supply products at fixed prices for future delivery, fears a rise in prices.
● A ship-owner who has chartered his vessels at a fixed time charter rate for the next six months, fears a fall in prices.
● An importer who needs to make an agreed payment in dollars in future, fears a drop in the value of his own currency.

● A company holding stocks of unsold products or materials, fears a drop in prices.

● An investor intending to invest £1 in a fixed-interest security in two months time, fears a drop in interest rates (and a rise in security prices).

In each case a drop (or rise) in commodity prices, security prices, currency values or interest rates could lead to a future loss. In some cases the precise nature of the risk is known, because of the details of a contract. In others, the exact size of the risk is not known. A futures market helps to reduce the risk and we now need to see how it is done.

We can take two different, though simple, examples. In the first case (Example A), a manufacturer has bought stocks of raw material and fears that prices will fall. In the second case (Example B), a corporate Treasurer has a million dollars to invest two months ahead. In the first example the risk is covered by the *sale* of futures (this is known as a *short* hedge). In the second example, it is covered by the purchase of futures (a *long* hedge).

Example A   The manufacturer's normal transactions are shown under the 'physical market' column in the table below. His subsequent transactions in the futures market, to protect himself against loss, arising from a fall in prices, are shown in the 'futures market' column:

	Physical Market	**Futures Market**
March 1	Makes a fixed contract to buy 1,000 tonnes of cocoa at £1,500 per tonne.	Sells 1,000 tonnes of cocoa at £1,510 for delivery in June.
June 1	Sells 1,000 tonnes of cocoa at £1,490.	Buys 1,000 tonnes of cocoa at £1,490 for the *spot* month (i.e. June).
	Loss of £10,000	*Profit of £20,000*

Example B

A corporate Treasurer, knowing he will have $1 million to invest in fixed-interest deposits in two months time, wishes to avoid receiving less because of an expected fall in interest rates. So he undertakes the futures contracts shown in the second column:

	Cash Market	**Futures Market**
January 1	Treasurer will have $1 million to invest on March 1. Current interest rate is 10% pa on Euro-dollar deposit.	Buys a March 3-month Euro-dollar deposit futures contract at 90, reflecting interest rate of 10% pa.

| March 1 | Treasurer invests $1 million in 3-month deposit at 8% pa. | Sells a March 3-month Euro-dollar futures contract at 92, reflecting interest rate of 8% pa. |
| | *Notional Loss: $5,000* | *Gain: $5,000* |

New Facilities

The above two examples are the simplest of the transactions now possible in the futures markets. The complexities of both futures and options already fill books, conference halls and seminars. Let me try to sketch in briefly, therefore, what direction some of the uses of the option and futures markets are now taking:

(i) Options on Futures   In the case of commodities it is already possible to take out options on certain commodity futures such as cocoa, coffee, and raw sugar. Similar developments were once thought likely in the currency field, though the existence of a high-turnover foreign exchange market, with built-in forward transactions for the main currencies, might inhibit these developments.

(ii) Options in Currencies   The option markets in currencies began as 'customised' foreign exchange currency options, a modified facility offered to individual customers by the big international banks through the foreign exchange market. They were clearly attractive. Corporate customers were getting what amounted to a personal service, options being written for sums and dates which exactly matched the customer's needs. The banks who wrote such specialised options, however, naturally saw it differently, since these and other option operations were unlikely to match and this often exposed the banks to unwanted risks. These anxieties naturally increased the interest in the development of 'traded' (standardised) foreign currency options first in Philadelphia, and then for a time in London. LIFFE's currency options and exchange-traded currency contracts are at present suspended.

(iii) International Linkages   All these markets are going international, partly reflecting business trends and opportunities, partly to attract the essential turnover. The clear aim is to develop 24-hour markets in futures and options. Markets in North America, Europe and the Far East are linking, or considering linking, their operations. This implies (a) adopting similar instruments and (b) allowing positions on one exchange to be offset on another. So far links have been forged between (i) London and New Zealand (wool futures); (ii) Amsterdam, Montreal, Vancouver and Sydney (commodity options); (iii) Chicago and Singapore (commodity, currency and security futures); (iv) London and Tokyo (financial futures); (v) New York and Sydney (gold futures).

LIFFE (London International Financial Futures Exchange)

Trading in financial futures began in London in September 1982. Financial options were first listed in 1985 and the exchange now has the most comprehensive range of financial futures and options in the world.

LIFFE has 180 members representing many sectors of the international financial community. They trade LIFFE's contracts by 'open outcry' on the exchange's trading floor and also on its Automated Pit Trading (APT) system. APT was launched by LIFFE in November 1989 as a means of extending the trading day beyond floor trading hours.

An 'open outcry' deal on this exchange takes place as follows:

● An order (to buy or sell a futures contract) is telephoned from a member's office to its booth on the trading floor. An order slip is made out and time-stamped.

● A runner in a *gold jacket* gives the order slip to a trader in the pit.

● The trader (in a *scarlet jacket*, business suit or jacket unique to his company) gives his order by open outcry and may use officially approved hand signals.

● Details of the executed order are put on the order slip and confirmed with the customer.

● A clearing slip is drawn up and sent to a central point to be entered on a computerised matching system. The confirmed deals will appear on company screens and unmatched deals are published regularly on the floor and rectified before the end of the day's dealings.

LIFFE is likely to be merged with the London Traded Options Market (LTOM) to form a new exchange, the London Derivatives Exchange, with a combined membership, single board and unified management, by the end of 1991.

13. Baltic Exchange

London has been a trading port for centuries, at least since the Romans confirmed it as a major crossing point on the Thames. Goods were naturally exchanged, and needed to be financed and insured. And the river, and the nearby estuary, brought ships.

So the proximity of the Baltic Exchange, Lloyd's Register of Shipping and the General Council of British Shipping, within a stone's throw of Lloyd's, hosts of foreign banks and London's commodity markets, is hardly a chance development. Shipping remains at the centre of the City's commercial activities.

What it Does

The place where this is most manifest is the high ceilinged, marble-pillared trading floor of the Baltic Exchange in St. Mary Axe. This is where the world's traders come to find a ship for their goods or goods for their ships; where second-hand ships are bought and sold; where air freight and spare aircraft capacity are married together; and where grain and other commodities are sold and new futures markets flourish.

The Baltic is primarily concerned with tramp shipping, that is with vessels which are not on scheduled services and are therefore available for hire. The Exchange brings together, directly or indirectly, the owners or operators of ships available for hire and charterers or hirers who wish to use them to take goods between agreed destinations at mutually agreed prices. These agreements are usually made voyage by voyage (or series of voyages) or over specified periods of time.

Thus firms with goods or commodities to shift round the world, either single cargoes or regularly, will use the Baltic to discuss what ships are available. Coal producers and their shippers will go there to find ships to transport coal from Hampton Roads and Richards Bay in the US to South Japan. Equally shippers of grain will look for vessels to ship it from the US Gulf to Antwerp.

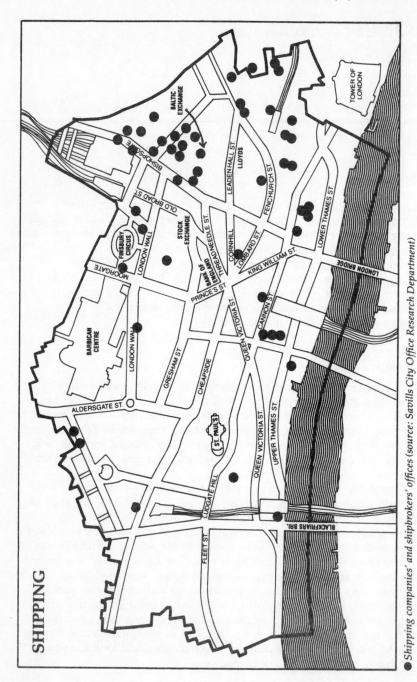

SHIPPING

Shipping companies' and shipbrokers' offices (source: Savills City Office Research Department)

What it is

The Baltic Exchange is an organisation providing its members with premises, facilities and agreed rules of conduct to enable them to undertake shipping, commodity and other related activities. Just like the Stock Exchange and Lloyd's, its origins lie in the coffee houses of the seventeenth century, where the ships' captains and merchants met to arrange cargoes or ships.

Two particular coffee houses attracted the shipping fraternity, the Jerusalem Coffee House and the Virginia and Maryland Coffee House. The latter subsequently became known as the Virginia and Baltic to reflect the two areas of the world bringing most business. After further expansion the 'Baltic' emerged in 1810, produced 'Baltic Club' regulations in 1823 and built its present trading floor in 1903.

The Baltic is now made up of over 600 corporate members, with 2,000 individual members of all nationalities. Some members are chartering agents representing merchants who have cargoes to move round the world. Others are owners' brokers, representing the shipowners. In other cases the merchants and shipowners may be members themselves. Some company members will have both owners' brokers as well as chartering agents under the same roof.

The Baltic International Freight Futures Market (BIFFEX), trading dry bulk cargo freight futures, which opened in 1985, is based on the Baltic Freight Index (BFI) published daily by the Baltic Exchange. The BFI shows the weighted average freight rate level and weighted average trip time charter hire level each day in the dry bulk cargo shipping market.

In July 1987 the Corn Exchange moved to the Baltic Exchange and conducts its trading business on the floor each Monday.

The motto of the Baltic is 'Our word, our bond'.

How it Works

Thousands of vessels are at this moment plying the world's oceans. Many have no idea, on arrival at their destination, where they will go next. More often than not, that decision is being decided for them on the Baltic or in one of the offices nearby.

Why the delay, you may ask. The truth is that shipping is fraught with obstacles, both God- and man-made. If a ship is delayed for an hour or a day that is going to cost someone money somewhere. So it is clearly better to delay final decisions on the next movement of a ship until it is clear that it is able—and free—to go there. The delay, however, simply makes the Baltic more essential than ever. (Or is it simply that because the Baltic exists, the delay in fixing the next leg of a tramp ship's journey is possible?)

As, say, a vessel sails towards Tokyo (or Sydney or Rio de Janeiro), the owners, or their brokers, will be moving on to the floor of the Baltic to secure the next round of business—from Tokyo to where? So will the brokers of other shipowners with ships bound for Tokyo.

At the same time Japanese steel mills may have cargoes they want moved from Tokyo to Los Angeles or Melbourne. Car manufacturers will have regular export shipments to arrange. Much of this information can be circulated by telephone, telex or printed circular. But the face-to-face meeting between noon and 2.00 p.m. on the Baltic can be crucial.

The reason is that some of the details, relating to either cargoes or ships, are highly competitive with other ships and cargoes. So the seeking out of the half dozen likely brokers on the floor and the beginnings of the next essential steps, offers and counter-offers, are naturally done personally.

Once details have been exchanged between one broker and another, an 'indication' is given of the kind of deal contemplated, but it is left to the two principals, the owners, to begin to specify details of a 'firm offer' and a 'firm counter-offer'.

These will contain details of cargoes and ships (fuel consumption, speed, freight charges, when the vessel is available, etc.: the list seems endless) and eventually lead to the drawing up of what is known as a 'charterparty' (from the Latin *carta partita*, 'divided paper', indicating the two parts of such an agreement). Once agreement is reached, the ship concerned is 'fixed'.

These 'fixtures' often begin on the floor of the Baltic, but rarely are all negotiations concluded there. So, like other City markets, a combination of an open market place, electronic and telephonic communications and administrative back-up produce the international business the Exchange depends upon.

International Flavour

The essential element remains the presence of so many foreign shipowners and merchants (or their agents or brokers) in the Square Mile. The British merchant fleet is now a more modest proportion of the world's total, but the agents and brokers of the bigger shipowning nations (whether traditional, new or simply flags of convenience) continue to have a presence in London.

Less than 10 per cent of the deals initiated or negotiated on the Baltic involve a British shipowner, importer, exporter or even crew. Yet up to 60 per cent of all dry cargo business 'fixed' on the world's open markets will be done by a Baltic member. And over 50 per cent of the sales of ships negotiated world-wide on the open market will be arranged through a Baltic member.

Ship broking is also conducted in other trade centres such as New York, Oslo, Tokyo, Hamburg, Rotterdam, Paris and Brussels. But in virtually every case, turnover is dominated by national, rather than international, requirements. London still manages to attract the bulk of the international business. Neither Tokyo nor New York are open for business at the same time; yet, because of London's time zone, both can and do manage to conduct business with London at each end of the day. And, cementing these international relationships, many of the Baltic's corporate members have their headquarters outside the UK. The International flavour of the Baltic Exchange is reflected in the invisible export earnings of its members, producing currently in excess of £400 million per annum for the UK balance of payments.

14. What The City Is

We began this small book with a brief outline of where and how the different City specialisations had developed and we summarised what the City of London did as a whole. Individual chapters have tried to explain how each sector works. In this penultimate chapter, we will attempt to sum up the City's main characteristics and to assess what kind of a financial centre the City now is.

Three main features seem to stand out:

● While servicing the British economy, London concentrates on *international* financial services.
● London offers a *wider variety* of services than other comparable financial centres.
● London is basically a *wholesale* centre in international finance, attracting deposits and business from other centres.

International Services

London's foreign earnings are now well documented. At the last official count, what are known as invisible earnings from Britain's financial services (they include the direct earnings from services to foreigners as well as the return on overseas investments) amounted to £6,184 million net in 1989, having reached close on £10,000 million in 1986. The details are shown in the table on page 108.

These are large figures by any standards, but they do not bring out how London, say, compares with New York, Zurich, Paris, Tokyo, etc. To do this, we need to look at each sector of the City separately.

(a) **Banking** London is running neck and neck with Tokyo in the proportion of international banking transitions it undertakes. Latest figures (end 1989):

	%
Tokyo	21.2
London	19.7
New York	9.7
Paris	6.5
Zurich	5.7
Frankfurt	3.7

(Source: *Bank for International Settlements*)

(b) Foreign Banks   There are now 526 foreign banks represented in London, compared with about 350 in New York. The London total includes 59 American banks and 53 Japanese. There are more American banks in London than in New York. (Source: *Bank of England*.)

The establishment of the European Bank for Reconstruction and Development in London, with some 40 countries as shareholders, consolidates London's pre-eminence.

(c) Foreign Exchange   We referred to the size of the turnover in London's foreign exchange market earlier and put it at some $187 billion a day. How does this compare with other world centres? The Bank of England, US Federal Reserve and the Bank of Japan have made these estimates:

	$ bn
London	187
New York	129
Tokyo	115
Zurich	57
Singapore	55
Hong Kong	49

(d) Insurance   Since so many countries insist on undertaking their own insurance and since domestic insurance is naturally undertaken by domestic firms in some of the largest markets, such as West Germany and the US, international business needs to be assessed separately. The total of insurance premiums available to international insurance firms is estimated at between $50 billion and $100 billion annually. Of this London is thought to account for the largest share.

(e) Gold   The turnover of the London gold market was estimated in an earlier chapter at between $1 and $2 billion a week. No official figures exist. The two leading world centres for *spot gold* remain London and Zurich, in this proportion:

City of London's Foreign Earnings[1] 1946–1989

	1946[2] £m	1956[2] £m	1963[2] £m	1965[3] £m	1968 £m	1986 £m	1988 £m	1989 £m
Insurance total[4]	20–25	70	85	81	198	4,260	3,515	2,927
Companies					90	1,871	1,958	1,677
Lloyd's					74	1,736	999	660
Brokers					34	710	690	721
Banking (net)[5]	5–10	25–30	45–50	82.5	67	2,295	780[5]	–(678)[5]
Commodity trading	5–10	25–30	20–25	80–90	57	572	631	728
Brokerage total	10	15–20	20–25	30–35	22	424	—	—
Baltic Exchange					33	221	334	427
Investment trusts					35	188	263	441
Pension funds					5	638	475	765
Unit trusts					2	175	155	218
Securities dealers						552	1,089	1,220
Money market brokers							56	73
Others						50	58	63
TOTAL	40–55	135–150	170–185	250–290	419	9,375	7,356	6,184

1 Including Edinburgh
2 Unofficial estimates by William M Clarke
3 From *Britain's Invisible Earnings* (report of the Committee on Invisible Exports, London, 1968)
4 Totals do not add because of direct investment income due to overseas parent companies
5 The official figures record the interest paid by banks on foreign currency borrowed overseas and lent to other UK residents. Excluding this, the figures for 1988 and 1989 would be £4,758m and £6,245m respectively

	%
London	40
Zurich	30

(Source: *London market estimates*)
(*Note*: In the case of *gold futures*, the New York COMEX exchange still dominates world transactions.)

(f) **Stock Exchange Turnover**   In terms of *domestic* turnover the London Stock Exchange ranks fourth, below Tokyo, (and Osaka) and New York. As a result the latest rankings by total turnover are as follows:

1989 (£m)	Fixed Interest	Equity	Total
1. Tokyo	605,402	2,639,965	3,245,367
2. Osaka	580,916	2,195,644	2,776,560
3. New York	860,682	1,800,649	2,661,331
4. London	190,987	507,159	698,146
5. Paris	252,581	226,671	479,252
6. Milan	309,942	105,622	415,564

(Source: *London Stock Exchange*)

If, however, turnover in *foreign equities* is taken as the measuring rod, London's total (the last annual figure was £40 billion) was nearly one and a half times that of New York and ten times that of Tokyo. The London total was nearly half of measured global foreign equity turnover.

(g) **International Equity Listings**   If the number of foreign company listings is compared, London is the leading centre for equities:

London	552
Frankfurt	352
Zurich	249
Amsterdam	236
Paris	229
Tokyo	121
New York	95

(Source: *London Stock Exchange*)

(h) **Euro-currency and Euro-bond Markets**   For a time London took the lion's share of the world's Euro-currency market, largely because the market had developed there. Although Tokyo is now just ahead of London on international banking transactions (see paragraph (a) above), Tokyo's lead is heavily based on foreign currency transactions with

Japanese residents. In terms of outstanding cross-border business alone, London's share remains the larger. As for Euro-bond business, some 65 per cent of primary issues have taken place in London in recent years. Most Euro-dollar, Euro-yen, Canadian dollar and Australian dollar Euro-bonds are issued out of London.

(i) Fund Management Both London and Edinburgh are acting as fund managers for domestic and international investments. UK institutional investors alone have assets of some £450 billion. In 1988, for example, some $16 billion of US pension fund foreign assets were managed in London and Edinburgh.

(j) Shipping Freight The Baltic Exchange claims that London accounts for between a half and two thirds of international shipping freight 'fixtures', and about 50 per cent of the market for sale and purchase of ships worldwide.

Variety of Services

Both the individual chapters and the above assessment of London's international services bring out the wide variety of different services available to foreign customers. Basically, London is offering banking and investment services, insurance and re-insurance, commodity dealings, shipping transactions and accountancy and legal advice on a world-wide basis.

This stands in contrast to other international centres which tend to concentrate on a narrower range of services. New York, for example, is strong on banking, investment, insurance and professional (i.e. accountancy and legal) advice, but lacks London's strength in shipping and commodities, while Chicago dominates in commodities and futures transactions. Zurich is strong on banking, investment, gold and insurance. Tokyo is prominent in banking and investment.

Wholesale Centre

London, like New York, has become almost a wholesale centre in financial services. By this we mean that in several areas, London and New York are attracting business from other financial centres. In the case of the City alone, it can be said that Singapore, Nassau, Bahrain and Hong Kong, for example, normally channel a significant amount of their financial business to London.

The best examples are:

(i) Re-insurance The capacity of the London insurance market, made up of Lloyd's and the insurance and re-insurance companies, is so great that large risks accepted and arranged in other centres will to a large extent be re-insured in London. A new re-insurance bourse, supported by 20 major insurance companies, is opening in London in 1991. Countries which have nationalised their own insurance companies often re-insure their domestic risks, or a significant share of them, in London.

(ii) Euro-currency   While large international projects may well be arranged in regional centres such as Hong Kong or Singapore, the funds to finance them can often be sought in London. At the same time, local Euro-currency deposits from centres such as Singapore, running into billions of dollars, will also be deposited in London.

(iii) Shipping Fixtures   The Baltic Exchange will naturally attract shipping fixtures relating to British trade with South America, Africa and the Far East. In addition, shipowners in Tokyo, Los Angeles or Rio de Janeiro will seek cargoes in London for journeys that do not touch British shores.

(iv) Commodities   London's commodity markets attract business between commodity producing countries and third countries. It is estimated that this often accounts for half London's commodity turnover.

Foreign Exchange   Banking demand in London to finance international banking transactions brings non-British business to the foreign exchange market. The depth of the London exchange market also attracts arbitrage business from all over the world.

World Competition

London has been competing in the world financial market for centuries. In the eighteenth century, the main competitor was Amsterdam. In the nineteenth century, Paris and Berlin were the main competitors. In the twentieth century, New York was added to the list.

Since 1945, New York and Zurich have been in the forefront of the competition, with Paris and Frankfurt reviving in the past two decades, along with regional newcomers in Tokyo, Singapore, Hong Kong and Nassau. Why has London remained so competitive so long? Several basic advantages have been maintained, as well as two fundamental postwar characteristics. The main advantages are:

   (i) Political stability.
   (ii) Good communications (airlines and telecommunications).
   (iii) Time-zone (ability to deal with Far East and North America on same day).

(iv) Compactness (all markets within a Square Mile).
(v) Free economic and financial system.
(vi) Competition encouraged (large numbers of foreign banks, security houses, shipping firms and insurance companies).
(vii) Swift decisions (big deals based on trust or word of mouth).
(viii) World contacts (political and Commonwealth links maintained in post-war world).

In addition, London has managed to maintain two essentials since 1945: the provision of money and continuing innovations.

Provision of Money

For a century and a half after the Napoleonic wars, London and the world was based on sterling. London could thus provide both money and financial services.

As the pound weakened in the 1940s and 1950s, London's sterling capital market began to dry up. It was at that precise moment that the City actively developed the Euro-currency market and thus managed to replace the provision of pounds with the provision of Eurocurrencies, i.e. other countries' currencies.

So although sterling finance is now well below dollar finance and probably, Deutschemark and yen finance, London-based banks can supply Euro-currencies of all kinds to support London-based services.

Innovation

Changes in the international financial markets have been quickening in the past decade. Innovation has spread quickly across frontiers. Technology has helped some of the changes; it has precipitated others. Legislation too (or its removal) has helped to change the structure of markets. These changes are still developing. London must keep pace if it is to maintain its competitive edge.

In the post-war period, London has produced several major innovations:

(i) New air-freight market on Baltic Exchange (1949).
(ii) Development of the Euro-currency and Euro-bond markets (1958–60).
(iii) Development of inter-bank wholesale market (1965–75).
(iv) Unlisted securities market on Stock Exchange (1979–80).
(v) Venture capital for small businesses (1976–84).
(vi) Insurance cover for nuclear plants, satellites, industrial complexes.
(vii) Finance packages for international projects.

(viii) New international financial futures market: LIFFE (1982).
(ix) New futures markets—petroleum, freight, etc. (1981–85).
(x) New options markets (Stock Exchange and LIFFE).
(xi) Development of new Euro-currency techniques such as swaps, FRNs, RUFs and NIFs.

Future Changes

The biggest changes at present seem to be taking place in banking and in the futures and security markets. Controls on banking have been and still are under review in Britain, the USA, Australia and Japan. Big structural changes in stock markets have taken place in London and Tokyo. And the European Community is planning to create an internal financial market, free of restrictions, with open access to banks and financial institutions operating in member countries, by 1992.

As a result, the following broad changes will now bear watching:

(i) The development of financial supermarkets, i.e. large groups providing a variety of services including banking, insurance, commodities and investment. This may lead to the gradual breakdown of barriers between different specialisations. Unlike the US and Japan, where such barriers seem to be breaking down, there is no statutory division in London between deposit banking and securities underwriting.

(ii) Moves towards 24-hour global trading in securities, commodities, futures, options, etc. by the establishment of firms in, or linkage of groups between, leading regional financial centres.

(iii) The development of new technologies providing global information, the transfer of money and the ability to deal in a variety of instruments and commodities. This will eventually have a profound impact on the trading floors of leading financial and commodity markets.

As we begin to peer towards the next century, these basic influences are increasingly changing the face of London, New York and Tokyo. Much bigger trading units are evolving, capable of undertaking a variety of different services on a global basis. Trading floors are giving way to video-screens. Individual financial centres are becoming more and more international. A world in which it will be possible to deal in most securities, commodities, options and other financial instruments twenty four hours a day is getting nearer. London at least is competing as vigorously as ever in this rapidly changing climate.

Global Trading in Foreign Exchange, Securities and Futures

What foreign exchange dealers have been doing for decades, security and futures traders are at last beginning to emulate. Global, 'round-the-clock' trading is spreading rapidly into different markets and different market places.

Investors' needs, reflecting the internationalisation of businesses, have coincided with two other phenomena: an increase in world communications (via satellites) and technology, and the de-regulation of financial markets. As a result, financial institutions are preparing themselves for global trading, in a variety of instruments, throughout 24 hours:

● In the case of *foreign exchange dealings* (see Chapter 8 and Map A) these have straddled the world's time zones for some time, with London lying comfortably in the middle. London begins to deal before Tokyo has closed. As the map shows, New York and Los Angeles begin to deal in the middle of London's peak activity. They have an incentive to begin early and, when the exchanges are extremely active, dealers in New York and Los Angeles have been known to begin at 5 a.m. local time to coincide with London dealings.

● Since the introduction of the 'Big Bang' in London (see Chapter 4 and Map B) and recent changes in security dealings in Tokyo, global *trading in international securities* has been increasing— helped by satellite communications and new technology. Dealing times on individual stock exchanges are beginning to lengthen (in London, in New York and in Continental centres) in order to facilitate truly global transactions.

● Dealings in commodities have straddled the globe for decades. But only in recent years have *futures transactions* (see Chapter 12 and Map C) begun to expand rapidly, linking one centre with another. Financial futures and options have added to these needs. As traditional markets (in Chicago, London and New York) and new markets (in Sydney, Montreal and Vancouver) have moved more closely together, global transactions have become more feasible.

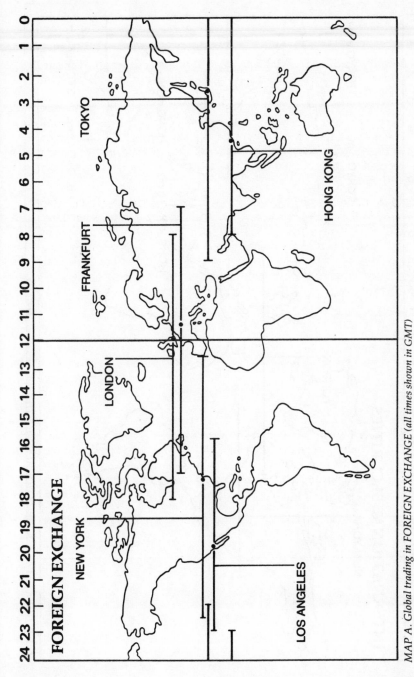

FOREIGN EXCHANGE

NEW YORK

LONDON

FRANKFURT

TOKYO

HONG KONG

LOS ANGELES

MAP A. Global trading in FOREIGN EXCHANGE (all times shown in GMT)

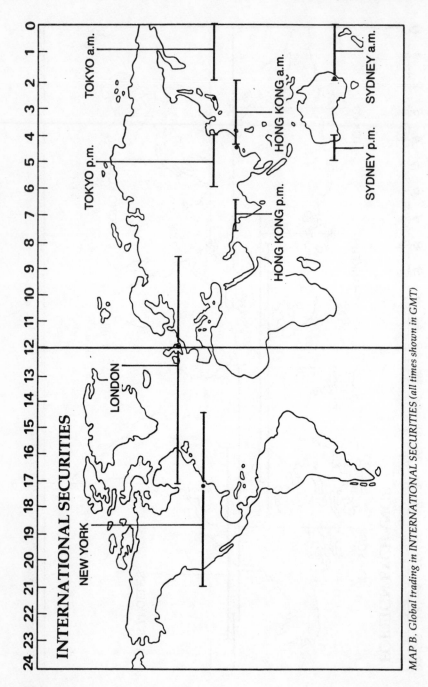

MAP B. *Global trading in INTERNATIONAL SECURITIES (all times shown in GMT)*

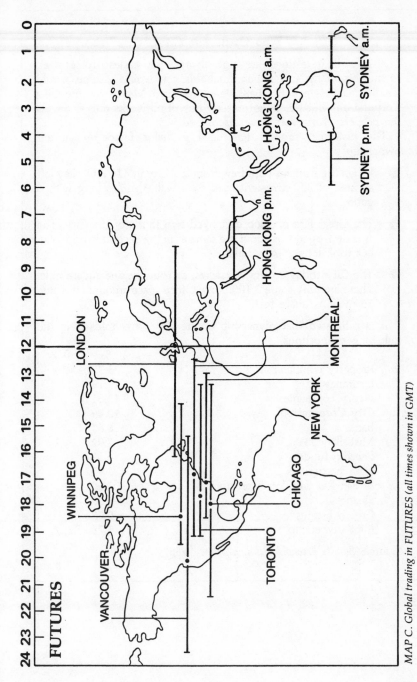

MAP C. Global trading in FUTURES (all times shown in GMT)

117

Who Owns The City?

The obvious questions are not always the easiest to answer. Ownership of the City's main freeholds, one would assume, would be divided between the banks and the Lord Mayor (or the City Corporation). But this is not exactly how it all works out, as Savills the property surveyors have discovered.

The historical process has been a major factor in current ownership:

● When the Romans withdrew from the City in 410 AD, they left an area of 330 acres enclosed by a wall $3\frac{1}{4}$ miles long with 6 gates.

● The Great Fire of 1666 destroyed two thirds of the City. The area destroyed was about the same as in the Second World War, but took longer to rebuild.

● The City today covers 667 acres, or roughly one square mile. There are now some 3,100 plots. Office space amounts to some 56 million square feet.

It is estimated that ownership of the City's freeholds is in the following proportions:

	%
Property companies	23.77
Insurance	19.19
Livery companies	12.61
City Corporation	10.49
Banks	8.81
Miscellaneous	7.92
Pension funds	6.69
Church/charities	3.90
British Rail/London Transport	2.00
Financial	2.00
Crown Estates	0.78
Joint ownership	1.78

(Source: *Savills Freehold Analysis, June 1985*)

15. How The City is Controlled

Financial markets should not be a free for all. The markets themselves need guidelines in order to function, safely and efficiently. Users of the markets, whether small investors or professional institutions, need protection from fraud and malpractice. And the public sometimes needs reassurance that such markets are broadly in the public interest. So efficiency, protection and public policy have all been involved in building up the regulations for the City's financial markets.

In the days when traditional institutions, such as the merchant banks or stockbroking firms, were undertaking the bulk of the City's financial business, a combination of self-regulation, a limited statutory framework and Bank of England 'nods and winks' were sufficient to keep the City reasonably under control. But as markets broadened, newcomers were introduced and new instruments and technologies began to spread, the need for stricter supervision grew stronger. A few frauds and collapses underlined the need for change. So, following a report from Professor Gower (in 1982) a White Paper (in 1985) and a Parliamentary debate, the new Financial Services Act was passed in 1986 and a new Banking Act in 1987.

Most of the present regulations were introduced on 29 April 1988 when the Financial Services Act of 1986 finally came into operation. This introduced the Securities and Investments Board (SIB) which, in turn, not only recognised five Self-Regulatory Organisations (SROs), but also provided a framework for the regulation of investment businesses. See the chart on page 120.

The SIB is a strange mixture:

- It is accountable to the Secretary of State for Trade and Industry and to Parliament.
- It has regulatory powers, can take offenders to Court and can carry out criminal prosecutions.
- It is a private limited company and is financed by the private sector, i.e. the City institutions.

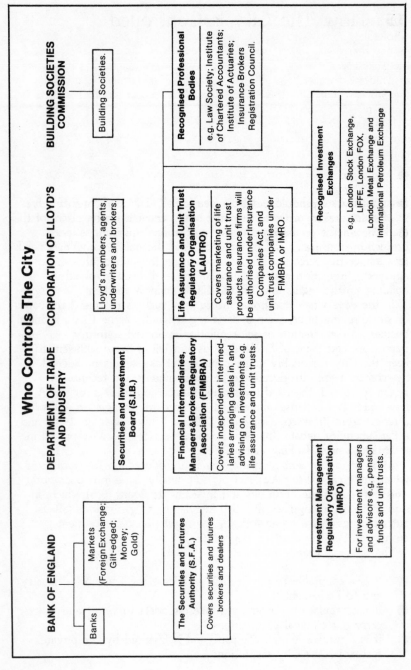

Who Controls The City

BANK OF ENGLAND

- Banks
- Markets (Foreign Exchange; Gilt-edged; Money; Gold)

The Securities and Futures Authority (S.F.A.)

Covers securities and futures brokers and dealers.

DEPARTMENT OF TRADE AND INDUSTRY

Securities and Investment Board (S.I.B.)

Financial Intermediaries, Managers & Brokers Regulatory Association (FIMBRA)

Covers independent intermediaries arranging deals in, and advising on, investments e.g. life assurance and unit trusts.

Investment Management Regulatory Organisation (IMRO)

For investment managers and advisors e.g. pension funds and unit trusts.

CORPORATION OF LLOYD'S

Lloyd's members, agents, underwriters and brokers.

Life Assurance and Unit Trust Regulatory Organisation (LAUTRO)

Covers marketing of life assurance and unit trust products. Insurance firms will be authorised under Insurance Companies Act, and unit trust companies under FIMBRA or IMRO.

Recognised Investment Exchanges

e.g. London Stock Exchange, LIFFE, London FOX, London Metal Exchange and International Petroleum Exchange

BUILDING SOCIETIES COMMISSION

Building Societies.

Recognised Professional Bodies

e.g. Law Society; Institute of Chartered Accountants; Institute of Actuaries; Insurance Brokers Registration Council.

Beyond the SIB (and its SRO's), regulation of City markets is also undertaken by the Bank of England (basically the banks and various wholesale markets such as foreign exchange, gold bullion and the money markets), Lloyd's (its own and insurance broking operations), the Take-Over Panel (for mergers and take-overs) and the Department of Trade and Industry itself which, in addition to being responsible for the SIB, also concerns itself with life assurance and breaches of the Companies Acts (insider dealings and fraud).

It is too soon to judge the success or failure of the new regulatory structure. But City discussions have already uncovered several major issues:

- The cost to the City of the whole structure (estimates range from £100 million to £300 million).
- The overlapping of the work of the SROs. One merger has already taken place; others may follow from experience.
- The impact of the rigid rules, and the corresponding paper work, on the competitive position of London, vis-à-vis New York etc.
- Whether the new structure will protect investors and prevent major financial failures in the City.